Selected Poems of James Henry

Introduction, editorial materials and arrangement
copyright © 2002 by Christopher Ricks

The moral right of the editor has been asserted.

This book was set in Adobe Garamond.

10 9 8 7 6 5 4 3 2 1

Library of Congress Cataloging-in-Publication Data

Henry, James, 1798-1876.
    [Poems]
    Selected poems of James Henry/edited by Christopher Ricks.
       p. cm.
    Includes index.
    ISBN 1-59051-021-6 (hardcover)
    1. Ricks, Christopher B. II. Title.

PR4785.H5 A6 2002
821'.8—dc21

                                                           2001059437

Selected Poems of
James Henry

edited by Christopher Ricks

HANDSEL BOOKS
an imprint of
Other Press • New York

Contents

The Life of James Henry

1798, 13 December. Born, the eldest of five children, at 15 College Green, Dublin, to Robert Henry, woollen-draper, and Katherine Olivia Henry, née Elder.

1804 Began education under Joseph Hutton, a Presbyterian and Unitarian.

1809 Bought for half-a-crown the Kilmarnock edition of Virgil.

1814 Entered Trinity College, Dublin.

1817 Scholar of the College.

1818, June. Wrote a poem "To the River Griese", "being the author's first rencontre with one of the Nine" (his musing note in 1866).

1819 Classical gold medal and B.A.

1822 M.A. and M.B. (Bachelor of Medicine) after five years studying medicine.

1823 Set up medical practice, soon successful, and became a Licenciate of the King and Queen's College of Physicians of Ireland.

1825 Fellow of the College of Physicians.

1826 Married Anne Jane Patton.

1827 Death of first-born child, Mary Jane.

1828 Death of second child, Ann Isabel.

1830 Birth of third child, Katharine Olivia (d. 1872). Published his first prose pamphlet, *A Letter to the Members of the Temperance Society*. [Other prose writings—satirical, argumentative, and allegorical—followed in 1838, 1840, 1841, 1842, 1851, 1860 and 1861.]

1832 M.D., his thesis being on miliary fever: *Miliaria accuratius descripta*. Elected vice-president of the College of Physicians.

1841 Began intense study of Virgil.

1845 On the death of his mother, received a large legacy and gave up the medical profession. Published his first Virgilian work, *The Eneis, Books I. and II. Rendered into English Blank Iambic*. [Other Virgiliana followed in 1848, 1851, 1853, and 1873, with posthumous publications 1877-1892.]

1846 Began his more than twenty years of journeying through Europe on foot, with his wife and his daughter Katharine, studying Virgilian manuscripts and rare editions.

1849 Death of his wife in Arco near Lake Garda, after an illness of ten days. The authorities refused a churchyard burial, so he effected her cremation in a tile-burner's kiln, and carried her ashes with him, back in the end to Ireland where they were buried with him in July 1876 (the gravestone, though, commemorating only Henry and his daughter Katharine).

1851 His first book containing poems, *The Unripe Windfalls in Prose and Verse of James Henry: [I] Miscellaneous Poems.* [Other books of poems followed in 1853, 1854, 1856, 1859, 1866, and, posthumously, 1877.]

1865 With his daughter, left Italy for Dresden.

1869 Returned to Ireland, and settled with his daughter at Dalkey Lodge, County Dublin, formerly his grandparents' and then his brother's home. Pursued his Virgilian commentary.

1872,December. Sudden death of his daughter Katharine. In October, he had written the dedication to her of the first fascicle (published 1873) of his commentary *Aeneidea*:

> To my beloved daughter, Katharine Olivia Henry, for twenty years - almost the whole of her adult life up to the present moment - ever beside me, at home and abroad, at the desk alike and in the public library, suggesting, correcting, advising, assisting, and cheering me on with all an affectionate daughter's zeal, solicitude, and devotion, I give, dedicate, and consecrate all that part of this work which is not her own.

1876, 14 July. Died at Dalkey Lodge. *18 July,* burial in Glendruid Cemetery.

Obituary by J. P. Mahaffy

The Academy, 12 August 1876

Dr. James Henry

On July 14, at Dalkey Lodge, the residence of his brother, this remarkable man closed an active and earnest life of seventy-eight years. His health of body and vigour of mind were unimpaired when a stroke of paralysis three months ago warned him that his labours must soon draw to a close.

Born in Dublin, James Henry was educated at first at a Unitarian school, and then sent to Trinity College. He was distinguished all through his course, was a scholar, and took his degree at the head of his class, with the classical gold medal, in 1818. He then adopted the medical profession, in which he soon attained great eminence and large practice, though his sceptical and independent ways of thinking estranged him from the religious and commonplace practitioners around him. His *Remarks on the Autobiography of Dr. Cheyne*, an exceedingly sarcastic and bitter exposition of the worldly advantages of Christianity, show clearly the nature of his opinions, and the boldness with which he expressed them. He even advanced to the shocking heresy that no doctor's opinion was worth a guinea, and accordingly set the example of charging five-shilling fees, an unheard-of thing in Dublin in that day. Though his sarcastic and trenchant tracts set him at war with the profession, his practice continued to increase, and he had realised some fortune when a large legacy made him completely independent of his ordinary work and induced him to lay aside professional controversies for literary pursuits.

He began (about the year 1848) to travel through Europe with his wife and only child, and to make researches upon his favourite author—Vergil. This occupation became an absorbing passion with him, and filled up the remainder of his life. After the death of his wife in the Tyrol (where he succeeded in cremating her and carrying off her ashes, which he preserved ever after) he continued to travel with his daughter, whom he brought up after his own heart, who emulated him in all his tastes and opinions, and who learned to assist him thoroughly and ably in his Vergilian studies. It was the habit of this curious pair to wander on foot, without luggage, through all parts of Europe, generally hunting for some ill-collated MS. of Vergil's *Aeneid*, or for some rare edition or commentator. Thus they came to know cities and libraries in a way quite foreign to the present hurrying age; they came to know all the men learned in their favourite subject, and all the librarians of the great libraries; in Florence, in Leghorn, in Dresden, in Heidelberg, in Dublin, these quaint and familiar figures will long be remembered. Seventeen times they crossed the Alps on foot, sometimes in deep snow, and more than once they were obliged to show the money they carried in abundance, before they were received into the inns where they sought shelter from night and rain.

During all these years—a full quarter of a century—they both pursued with unwearied diligence the criticism and exegesis of the text of the *Aeneid*. In his *Twelve Years' Journey through the Aeneid of Vergil* Dr. Henry first disclosed to the world that a great new commentator on Vergil had arisen, and those who will look through Conington's work will see how many of the best and most original notes are ascribed to Henry. He also printed privately (he never would publish anything except a few papers in periodicals) versified accounts of his travels, something like the Roman saturae or medleys, and other poems more curious than beautiful—some of them, however, striking enough from their bold outspokenness in religious matters.

Having thoroughly examined every MS. of the *Aeneid* of any value, he returned a few years ago to Dublin, when declining years disposed him to rest from travel, and where the library of Trinity College afforded him a rich supply of early printed books on his subject. Here he spent most of his time, hunting up obscure allusions, seeking new illustrations, and labouring to perfect that exegesis which he held to be the main problem in editing Vergil. For in textual criticism he had become thoroughly conservative: he believed in the pure condition and good preservation of the *Aeneid*, and used to scorn those scholars who emended because they could not understand. He was with difficulty persuaded to contribute some notes on passages to *Hermathena*, from commentary carried out on the same scale through the whole twelve books. This commentary is complete, and has been bequeathed, I believe, to the care of Mr. Davies, the well-known editor of the *Agamemnon* and *Choephori*, a thoroughly competent scholar, and an attached friend of the author. The MS. is in such beautifully clear and accurate writing that its publication will not be difficult. A fragment of 176 pages on the first twenty-six lines (*Eneidea*) was printed a few years ago by Dr. Henry, but he could not content himself with either his own work or the work of any known printer, and so preferred the postponement of the remainder till after his death. With all its ability, its originality, its acuteness, I fear this wonderful commentary is on too large a scale, and embraces too wide a range of illustrations and discussions, to find favour with our examination-driven students. It is like the work of a sixteenth-century scholar, of a man who studied and thought and wrote without hurry or care, who loved his subject and scorned the applause of the vulgar crowd. As such, and as the fullest and best exegesis ever attempted of Vergil, Dr. Henry's commentary cannot fail to take a permanent and unapproachable place.

To his personal friends the memory of the dear old man will stand out no less distinct and indelible. His long white locks and his somewhat fantastic fur dress, which gave him a certain Robinson Crusoe air, were combined with great beauty and vivacity of countenance and a rare geniality and vigour of discourse. There was a curious combination of rudeness and kindness, of truculence and gentleness, of severity and softness in him, which made him different from other men. He was so honestly outspoken about himself that he could hardly be offensive to others, and those who saw his deep and bitter grief ever since his daughter—the support of his age, and the hope of his future fame—was taken from him by sudden death know how keen and thorough were his affections. He never ceased thinking and talking of her, and looked with calmness and even with satisfaction upon his approaching death, though it afforded him no hope of meeting her again. It was an escape from the desolation of a life without her whom he had loved.

The following are his principal printed works, very few of which (if any) were published, and many of which are undated. They speak the history of his mind by their very titles:

Miliaria accuratius descripta. thesis habit in Univ. Dub., 1832; *An Account of the Drunken Sea*, Dub., 1840; *An Account of the Proceedings of the Government Police in the City of Canton*, Dub., 1840; *Dialogue between a Bilious Patient and a Physician*, Dub., (no date); [etc.]

— J. P. Mahaffy

[Sir John Pentland Mahaffy (1839-1919), provost of Trinity College, Dublin, 1914-1919; classical scholar devoted to ancient Greek life, literature, and history; "a remarkably versatile writer of great shrewdness and sagacity" (*The Concise Dictionary of National Biography*). Devout and a wit: ordained 1864; "Mahaffy, asked by a young man in a Dublin street if he was saved, paused and answered: 'I am, but between you and me, it was a damned close squeak'" (*Geoffrey Madan's Notebooks*).]

Introduction

"By what mistake were pigeons made so happy?"

Has there ever been a less mistaken, a more happy, entrance upon a poem? James Henry's opening line sets before you a vivid sense of the world at once darkened and lightened. Darkened, because if there is any happiness on this planet it must be taken for granted that this is despite the Maker and his providence; lightened, because of the endearing ruefulness. Moreover the opening is even better than my quotation of it, since Henry doesn't arrive at his question-mark at the end of the line (as it is quoted by me to help me to have a happy opening too), but only after the question has taken its affectionate time, has moved unhurriedly from *and* to *and* to *and*:

> By what mistake were pigeons made so happy,
> So plump and fat and sleek and well content,
> So little with affairs of others meddling,
> So little meddled with?

This is a poet who appreciates how much can be effected by the phrase "So little", a poet who can combine a direct vision of life with a turn that has its unexpected particularity of instance. Pigeons, for Heaven's sake. And this keeps its comedy touslingly alive to its very end.[1]

James Henry—Irish scholar and poet—not to be confused with

---

[1] For the poem, see p. 156.

Henry James, American novelist and man of letters… But it was the glint of comedy in the reversal of the names that first caught my eye. So let me move immediately to anecdote, even though—like hearsay—it is not evidence.

I was editing the *New Oxford Book of Victorian Verse*, and browsing in the stacks of the Cambridge University Library. And the name James Henry intrigued me with its suggestion of the literally and literarily preposterous. Taking down one of his many books from the shelf, I noticed a few things: that these poems of his had been printed (at his own expense, surely?) in Dresden, Germany; that he had inscribed and presented the copy to the Cambridge library; and—unkindest cut of all—that the pages had never been cut. "Unopened", as book dealers say. Intrigued, I took the book out, and wielded a paper knife. Straightaway I loved the way in which James Henry wielded words.

I put eight of his poems into the *New Oxford Book of Victorian Verse* (1987): "Out of the Frying Pan into the Fire", "Pain", "Old Man", "Very Old Man", "Another and another and another", "My Stearine Candles", "Once on a time a thousand different men", and "Two hundred men and eighteen killed".[2] It was a pleasure to see D.J.Enright promptly, promptedly, pick up "Pain" for his humorously glum anthology *Ill at Ease: Writers on Ailments Real and Imagined* (1989).[3]

---

[2] So, for an immediate chance to dissent from or assent to somebody's initial sense of Henry's merits, see pp. 54, 44, 80, 81, 87, 57, 100, 171.

[3] Subsequent to the *New Oxford Book of Victorian Verse*, Henry has also been included, to my delight and not mine alone, in Daniel Karlin's *Penguin Book of Victorian Verse* (1997), with four poems: "Breathe not a murmur"; "Man's Universal Hymn"; "The human skull is of deceit"; and "The son's a poor, wretched, unfortunate creature". In Valentine Cunningham's *The Victorians: An Anthology of Poetry & Poetics* (2000), with five: "The Roman Lyrist's soul, 'tis said", "Odds bobs, brother Tom, do you know, by the Powers", "I am a versemaker by trade", "Two hundred men and eighteen killed", and "I am the pink of courtesy". And in Paul Keegan's *New Penguin Book of English Verse* (2000), with two: "Another and another and another", and "The son's a poor, wretched, unfortunate creature".

Henry stayed in my mind. First, in his anticipation of Samuel Beckett's unrelenting permutation-games, which moved me to quote the thirty-five lines of "So father Adam was his own born son", a deftly obdurate poem of 1858, in *Beckett's Dying Words* (1993). Second, two of my earlier choices, "Very Old Man", and "Another and another and another", maintained their place in my eyes and entered, against stiffer competition, the *Oxford Book of English Verse* (1999). Third, in November 1999, the B.B.C. allowed me a twenty-minute talk on Henry's poems. Last, and most, there is this present opportunity for an ample selection from a poet whose poems have breathed only in oblivion, partly because, a century and a half ago, they were privately printed—and this mostly in Dresden and (posthumously) in Leipsig.

Did he ever once get reviewed? Apparently not. But this seems to have whetted, not fretted. There is a sly zest in his puncturing of the pseudo-punctilious, his "Letter received from a reviewer to whom the author, intending to send the MS. of his Six Photographs of the Heroic Times for review, had by mistake sent, instead of it, a MS. of Milton's Paradise Regained" (p. 91).

He was in his fifties and sixties when he hit his stride and his particular notes. He was the man in his mid-fifties whose life is in his face and is on the face of this book. But if he is now a neglected poet, there is nothing to choose between now and then, since he has always been neglected. Since I love his voice, I love the thought that it might at last be heard. We sometimes speak carelessly of a poet's work being revived; mistakenly, because it is not the work that is revived (in all the cases that matter it never died) but rather a body of readers that is at last revived or vived. Anyway, it is not a matter of reviving Henry's reputation as a poet. No such reputation was ever enjoyed by him.[4]

---

[4] Henry did not make it into the 19th-century listings in the *Cambridge Bibliography of English Literature* or the *New CBEL* (vol. 4, 1999). In the twelve volumes of the *Poets and the Poetry of the Nineteenth Century* (1891-7, 1905-7), Alfred Miles included

To this day his poems go unmentioned except by those who admire the scholar and the man—and from these, the poems get only shortish shrift.[5] For me, they are unaffectedly direct, sinewy, seriously comic. And brave. For it took courage in James Henry to avow so many pagan values and to repudiate most Christian—or religious—ones. Henry at one point wondered whether to include in one of his volumes on Virgil a comparison of Christianity and Paganism. "In favour of which?", asked his friend the classical scholar J.P.Mahaffy. "Of Paganism, of course", was the reply. "Then", said Mahaffy, "I would advise you to say nothing about it".[6]

What Henry does with his convictions is maintain them, with a syntax that will not be gainsaid or deflected: "Out of the Frying Pan into the Fire" (p. 54) unwinds fifty lines through one sentence—a death sentence, an eternal torment sentence, and then at the end the down-to-earth likelihood of a prison sentence. The momentum is

nearly five hundred poets; Henry was not among them. W. H. Auden and Norman Holmes Pearson, who had an eye and an ear for unacknowledged legislators, found no place for Henry in their five volumes, *Poets of the English Language* (1950). That Arthur Quiller-Couch in his *Oxford Book of English Verse* (1900) and Helen Gardner in her *New Oxford Book of English Verse* (1972) went without Henry goes without saying. The Irish might have been expected to notice Henry, but there is nothing by him in Donagh MacDonagh and Lennox Robinson's *Oxford Book of Irish Verse* (1959), in John Montague's *Faber Book of Irish Verse* (1974), in Thomas Kinsella's *New Oxford Book of Irish Verse* (1986), or in Seamus Deane's *The Field Day Anthology of Irish Writing* (1991), all four thousand pages of it.

[5] Even J.P. Mahaffy: 'versified accounts of his travels, something like the Roman saturae or medleys, and other poems more curious than beautiful'. Even John Richmond, whose subtitle begins 'Physician, Versifier, ...', and who says of the miscellaneous poems: 'Like nearly all of Henry's verse they have little or no poetic merit.' And even J.B.Lyons, whose chapter on the poems is headed 'Rhymer', and who says: 'Some titles will indicate the banalities a reader encounters' - then including in his list 'Out of the Frying Pan into the Fire'. See p. 54 and judge yourself whether this vision of divine judgment, of the fires of hell, is a banality.

[6] I owe this anecdote to Ian Jackson, via J. A. Richmond; the source is A. H. Sayce, *Reminiscences* (1923), p. 129.

momentous. More, it is characteristic of Henry that on quite a different occasion he should turn to the single sentence poem, this time in a deep anecdote of love and loving kindness: "I saw, in Dresden, on a windy day" (p. 161), a single sentence of eighteen lines that arrives, not at eternal torment, but at the generous gratification of "well pleased and happy". His vignette here captures a moment of the resourcefulness of human love, of man and woman in a loving God-free zone, the woman more simply compassionate than the man she loves. Like any good humanist, any true one, Henry liked human beings. He disliked superiority to them, as is clear from a resourcefully ironic poem, "Clever people are disagreeable" (p. 96), a poem that proceeds to ask you whether you don't sometimes find people of any kind disagreeable...

But not as disagreeable as the Christian God. Henry was not afraid to ask the ancient questions with immediate urgency. The problem of pain, for instance, or rather the problem of reconciling pain with a god who is all-powerful and all-loving, was not, for this doctor and sceptic, as easily assuaged as, oh, C.S. Lewis duly made out. "Pain" (p. 44) shows Henry's refusal to fob or be fobbed. But then he did not believe in any all-powerful all-loving god; if he had to choose between a God and gods, he preferred polytheism, but he believed that it would need either a miracle or a ruse for even polytheism to be humane. "Once on a time a thousand different men" (p. 100) imagines a very different solution, divining ignorance as bliss.

"I the Lord thy God am a jealous God". Henry's sense of the Christian God was that he was not so much jealous—zealous—as envious. And irritable. The poem on the Creation (p. 116), which became when he reprinted it the first of a series of Old-World Stories,[7] is aware that the Devil finds work for idle hands to do, and so can't help wondering whether among the idle hands there might not once have been the hands of God, God with not just time on his

[7] *Poems Chiefly Philosophical* (1856), but then reprinted as the first of the *Old-World Stories* in *Menippea* (1866), which is where it is placed in the present selection.

hands but eternity on them. The poem enters the lists at once:

On the day before the first day,
God was tired with doing nothing,
And determined to rise early
On the next day and do something.

So much for the beginning of time, divine and human. And the end? Henry, whose comedy is never far from tragedy, has three poems that contemplate the vistas of time, of age, of endlessness: "Old Man" (p. 80), which opens: "At six years old…"; "Very Old Man" (p. 81), which opens "I well remember how some threescore years / And ten ago…"; and "Another and another and another" (p. 87), which contemplates the unwelcome vista of eternity. What fills this lovely poem is a longing for oblivion, and this closer in its unyielding timbre to that of another remarkable Irishman, Samuel Beckett, than to the Keatsian or Tennysonian world-weariness. Time is the mercy of eternity, and death is the mercy of time. A mercy.

These last three poems are all from *Poems Chiefly Philosophical*, where "philosophical" means not only thinking things through but being philosophical about these perturbations of mind and spirit. Henry was at one with Oliver Edwards, who is eternized in Boswell's *Life of Johnson* (17 April 1778) for ungrumblingly rumbling, "I have tried too in my time to be a philosopher; but, I don't know how, cheerfulness was always breaking in".

Henry had integrity—intellectual, moral, political, and spiritual —so his work has an integrity, a consistency, for all its engaging diversity of topic and tone. The man who writes with such sardonic fervour about religion is manifestly the same person who has a vibrating indignation at political injustice and indifference; see the first poem in this selection, "Progress" (p. 38), and the last—on safety down the coal-mines—"Two hundred men and eighteen killed" (p. 171). But the ordinary daily things of this life are there for his

Muse and his amusement too; let us honour the man who invented chairs, say, or let us never cease to be grateful for the best of all lights, the stearine candle: "The commercial name of a preparation consisting of purified fatty acids, used for making candles". The first citation in the *Oxford English Dictionary* is 1839: "In June, 1825, M. Gay Lussac obtained a patent in England for making candles from margaric and stearic acids, improperly called stearine". Improperly be damned.

So let me end this introduction to the poems with the poem in which this opponent of religion, not just of organized religion, paid tribute to his personal Trinity. First, to Prometheus, for his stealing fire on our behalf. Second, to Athena, the goddess of wisdom, before whose shrine he will keep a lamp burning. And third, to the inventor of the best candles, stearine candles, invented a few decades before James Henry paid his tribute, a tribute that winds exquisitely to its final compliment, to the art of the candle and to art itself:

My Stearine Candles

He's gone to bed at last, that flaring, glaring,
Round, red-faced, bold, monopolizing Sun,
And I may venture from their hiding-place
To bring my pair of stearine candles forth
And set them, firmly stayed, upon my table,
To illuminate and cheer my studious evening.
Thou hast my praise, Prometheus, for thy theft,
And, were I to idolatry addicted,
Shouldst be my God in preference to Buddh,
Brahma, or Thor, or Odin, or Jove's self.
Her of the olive branch I'd hold to thee
The next in honor, and before her shrine
In gratitude would keep for ever burning

A lamp of such Athenian oil as Plato,
Demosthenes, Pythagoras, and Solon
Were wont in bed to read by, after midnight.
The third, last person of my Trinity
Should be th' inventor of the stearine candle;
He that enabled me to sit, the long
Midwinter nights, in study, by a light
Which neither flickers nor offends the nostrils,
Nor from the distance of a thousand miles,
Or thousand years, or both perhaps, keeps ever
And anon calling me - like some bold child
The mother's hand - to come and snuff and snub it;
But steady, cleanly, bright and inodorous,
Than tallow more humane, than wax less costly,
Gives me just what I want, and asks back nothing.

———————————

Some words on Henry's prose writings, swinging and swingeing. First, there are those that derive from his profession as a doctor, such as *A Letter to the Members of the Temperance Society, showing that the use of tea and coffee cannot be safely substituted for that of spirituous liquors, and proposing a rule of diet from which those substances are excluded* (1830), and *A Dialogue between a Bilious Patient and a Physician* (1838).

Second, the allegorical fables, some of them social (*An Account of the Drunken Sea*, 1840), most of them political: *An Account of the Proceedings of the Government Metropolitan Police in the City of Canton* (1840—for Canton read Dublin); and *Little Island and Big Island* (1841—on Ireland versus England). Henry was to tease out something of his Irishness in his poem *Thalia Petasata Iterum, or A foot journey from Dresden to Venice* (1877). Someone from the upper Rheinthal says to him, "and you're an Englishman". "Not badly guessed", said I, "though not quite right".

"A deep salt sea—
Alas! not broad enough—my little island
Divides from England...

I'm of that stock,
In Ireland born, by blood an Englishman,
But not by sympathy".

Third, relatedly, there is the Swiftian indignation: *Report of a Meeting of the Informers of Dublin held on the Sunday evening, Feb. 6th, 1842, being the day after the execution of John Delahunt for the murder of the boy Thomas Maguire* (1842).

Fourth, the freethinking sermons: *A Word about War* and *A Word about Judgment* (1842).

Fifth, the union of several passionate convictions, such as *Religion, Wordly-Mindedness [sic] and Philosophy, being Strictures on the Autobiography of the late John Cheyne M.D., and on his Essays on Partial Derangement of the Mind in Supposed Connexion with Religion* (1860). His anti-Christian crusade is dramatized as an unavailing theodicy in *Cain, a Soliloquy* (1856), appended to *Poems Chiefly Philosophical.* The most acute of these provocations is the *Dialogue between a Stethoscopist and an Unborn Child* (1854), which he published with *A Half Year's Poems* (1854) and which is included in this selection.

And then there is the work for which alone Henry's name tenuously but tenaciously survives: his commentary on Virgil.[8] Mahaffy for his part feared that "this wonderful commentary is on too large a scale, and embraces too wide a range of illustrations and discussions, to find favour with our examination-driven students". Or our examination-driven professors. But those of us who are not classical scholars, those alert to confirmation for their sense that in his poems Henry is intelli-

---

[8] For Henry's translations from Virgil, variously unsuccessful, see the excerpt in *Virgil in English* (ed. K.W. Gransden, Penguin Poets in Translation, 1996) and Gransden's introduction.

gently steely and far from naive, can profit happily, for instance, from the imaginative energy with which Henry creates a long imaginary conversation about the demerits of Conington's translation of Virgil.[9] Or for an unimaginary conversation (in which an imaginative scholar finds himself up against unimaginative librarians), there is Henry's account of how he was treated as a reader in the British Museum—as against in the royal library in Dresden where courtesy reigned:

> It was not long before I had the verso of this agreeable recto of one leaf of my library life. Returning from Dresden to Ireland through London, and calling at the library of the British Museum with a present of a recently published work of my own, I begged to be allowed to look at a passage in a volume which stood on a shelf close beside me. "Have you permission to read in the library?" asked the officer in charge. "No, I have not; nor have I come for the purpose of reading; nor do I intend to stay longer in London than this day. All I ask is permission to look at a few lines in that volume. I shall do so without sitting down or stirring out of this spot. I shall not require to have the book in my hands for quite five minutes". "You cannot be allowed; it is contrary to rule. But if you get a banker, or the principal of any college, seminary or commercial establishment in London, to write a letter to Sir Henry Ellis, certifying that you are a fit and proper person to read in the library, Sir Henry Ellis will, on receipt of such letter, post you a ticket of admission, and on that ticket you can come and read in the library daily for the next three months". "I do not want admission to the library; I am in it already. I only wish to have that book, there, in my hands for five minutes, and then to go away and trouble you no more". "Impossible; it is contrary to rule". "Can I see Sir Henry Ellis?" "Certainly". Sir Henry Ellis made his appearance, replied to my request in the same terms, and I proceeded to Ireland, more than ever convinced that even in civilization there is a golden mean, every step beyond which is a step further from humanity, and towards an extreme in which ingenuas didicisse fideliter artes *non* emollit mores

---

[9] *Aeneidea*, vol. I (1873), pp. 29-56: Book I. Parergon.

sed sinit esse feros,[10] and consoling myself *en vrai Darwiniste* as I am, with the prospect I saw opening in the distance for my successors, that books in British libraries continuing to be guarded as if they were Hesperides' apples, readers would in due course come to be born with the strength of Hercules, and the instinct to use it on the proper occasion.[11]

The sardonic acumen there is continuous with the comedy (rueful the day) of many a poem by Henry. A different continuity would relate the poems' humanity, at once simple and subtle, to Henry's being so moved—and moving us—at the death of Dido:

INGEMUIT REPERTA. —*Groaned deeply,* the sight of the light bringing back rapidly to her mind the troubles she had had in it. So rapidly does our author pass from point to point ("summa fastigia sequitur")[12] that the reader is left to make out for himself the delicate connexions. Tired and disgusted with the world as Dido is, she cannot die without taking a last view of that light in which she had once been so happy. The sight of the light, however, serves only to bring back with increased distinctness the recollection of her misfortunes; and with a deep groan she closes her eyes again and dies. It is the dying human being who OCULIS QUAESIVIT ALTO CAELO LUCEM; it is individual Dido who INGEMUIT. There is no so touching word in the whole Aeneid as this INGEMUIT, placing as it does before the mind capable of such sympathies the whole heart-rending history in a single retrospective glance. Show me anything at all like it in the Iliad.

Show me anything at all like Henry's best poems in Victorian poetry or anywhere, come to that.

---

[10] Modifying Ovid, *Ex Ponto* II ix 47-8: "Moreover to have conscientiously studied the liberal arts refines behaviour and does not permit it to be savage" (Henry: "does *not...but* permits it...").

[11] *Aeneidea*, vol. I (1873), Preface, pp.lxxvii-lxxviii.

[12] Modifying *Aeneid* i 342: "summed up in brief".

A Note on Metrics, Titles, and Composition

In some of his volumes (not his first, 1851, and not his last, posthumously, in 1877), Henry made use of marks to indicate a stress. In his *Notes of a Twelve Years' Voyage of Discovery in the first six Books of the Eneis* (1853), he set himself to justify the practice:

> It is much to be desired that even ordinary poetry were always printed with such helps, without which it is impossible for any one who has not a well practised poetical ear, to know where the ictus of the voice falls, in any measure which deviates, even in the slightest degree, from the accustomed jingle.

But the marks are a vexation, at once finicky and crude in that they do not intimate any degrees of stress but instead announce a single-minded insistence. The first poem in this selection, "Progress", opened in 1851:

> Yes; I'll believe in progress when I see you
> Battering old jails down, and not building new;
> When I behold you make but a beginning
> To sleep with open doors and unbarred windows.

When reprinted two years later, this became:

Yés; I'll belíeve in prógress whén I sée you
Báttering old jáils down, ánd not búilding néw;
Whén I behóld you máke but á begínning
To sléep with ópen dóors and únbarred wíndows.

Is not the first (unmarked) version the more open, the more accessible, even the more audible?

The present selection takes or exercises the liberty of removing such marks. This is not a mark of disrespect, or rather it respects the poems even more than it does the poet.

I saw, in Dresden, on a windy day,
A man and woman walking side by side,
—I tell a pláin fact, not a poet's story,

—the plainness of this unaffected opening was flecked by the poet's misguidedly assuming that the reader needs guidance, needs to have "plain" put pláinly.

Moreover, Henry himself betrays an unease as to just what the right markings would be. When first published in 1856, his poem on the Creation began with a stanza spattered with accent-marks:

Ón the dáy befóre the fírst day
Gód was tíred with dóing nóthing,
Ánd detérmined tó rise eárly
Ón the néxt day ánd do sómething.

When he reprinted the poem in 1866, this became:

Ón the dáy befóre the fírst day
God was tired with doing nothing,
And determined tó rise early
On the néxt day and do sómething.

All four marks have gone from the second line, as have five from the three lines that follow. Best for them all to go.

Henry often avails himself, as in those four lines, of a measure that, though frequent in classical literature, has been relatively rare in English: trochaics, the trochee being less cómmon whereas the iambic, which is more common in English verse, is secúre. Kenneth Haynes, in his edition of Swinburne's *Poems and Ballads & Atalanta in Calydon* (Penguin, 2000), has a note to "Stage Love":

> Trochaics are among the most enduring metres of classical poetry: Archilochus wrote in trochaics, the metre occurred regularly in Greek and Latin tragedy and comedy and also in late works like the *Pervigilium Veneris*, and it was used in goliardic verse.... Tennyson's "Locksley Hall" (1842), Longfellow's "The Song of Hiawatha" (1855), and Browning's "A Toccata of Galuppi's" (1855) were recent poems in trochaics.

Henry's characteristic movement is trochaics of four stresses ("God was tired with doing nothing"), and these not rhymed— whereas Blake, Tennyson and Browning, in the poems mentioned, all rhyme their trochaics. Though Longfellow does not rhyme in "The Song of Hiawatha", the movement of his lines is very different from that which Henry practised. For whereas Longfellow chose a sequence of end-stopped lines, end-punctuated even (of the first twenty lines of "Hiawatha", only one is without terminal punctuation), Henry often relished the swing on from one line to the next, the enjambment that loves using its legs. Feel the threaded movement from line to line here, the end of "Cain and Abel":

Like a knotless thread, my story
Here drops from between my fingers,
For what more Cain in the land of
Nod did, or elsewhere, 's not written.

———————————

Henry liked making play with Latin titles for his later volumes of English poems:

Thalia Petasata, or A foot-journey from Carlsruhe to Bassano (1859): The Muse [the one associated with comedy or light verse] in her Travelling [or Broadbrimmed] Hat. (*Thalia Petasata Iterum*, 1877, being the same Again).

Menippea (1866): Menippean Satires (Satires after the manner of Menippus).

Poematia (1866): Little Poems (or Short Poems).

In the present selection, the few words of Latin and Greek in the poems are glossed at the foot of the page.

———————————

Henry subscribed his poems with a place and a date; for instance, that on the Creation appends "Dalkey Lodge, Dalkey (Ireland), Jan. 21, 1855". These details have here been moved from the foot of the poem (where they might detract from or distract from the firmness of its ending), and are incorporated in the Index of Titles and First Lines, given under the title when the poem has one.

The Works of James Henry

Poems

*The Unripe Windfalls in Prose and Verse of James Henry: [I]
Miscellaneous Poems* [48 numbered leaves, 96 pages, later listed by
Henry as *Minor Poems*] (Dublin, 1851)

My Book [unnumbered pages, approx. 200, later listed by Henry as
Minor Poems] with *Six Photographs of the Heroic Times* [314 pages],
being a Metrical Translation of the first six Books of the Eneis
(Dresden, 1853)

A Half Year's Poems [154 pages] with *Dialogue between a
Stethoscopist and an Unborn Child* [14 pages] (Dresden, 1854)

[A translation of Henry's poems into German was made by Julius
Schanz: *Gedichte von James Henry* (Dresden, 1854)]

Poems Chiefly Philosophical [286 pages] (Dresden, 1856)

*Thalia Petasata, or A foot-journey from Carlsruhe to Bassano,
described on the way in verse* [188 pages] (Dresden, 1859)

Menippea [222 + vi pages] (Dresden, 1866)

Poematia [188 + x pages] (Dresden, 1866)

*Thalia Petasata Iterum, or A foot journey from Dresden to Venice,
described on the way in verse* [101 pages] (Leipsig, 1877)

On Virgil

The Eneis, Books I. and II. Rendered into English Blank Iambic, with New Interpretations and Illustrations (London, Dublin, and Edinburgh, 1845)

Commentaries on the First Two Books of the Eneis (London, 1848)

The Unripe Windfalls of James Henry: [III] Specimen of Virgilian Commentaries. [IV] Specimen of a New Metrical Translation of the Eneis (Dublin, 1851)

My Book [containing *Minor Poems* and *Six Photographs of the Heroic Times, being a Metrical Translation of the first six Books of the Eneis*] (Dresden, 1853)

Notes of a Twelve Years' Voyage of Discovery in the first six Books of the Eneis (Dresden, 1853)

Adversaria Virgiliana written for translation into German, and published in that language in the Göttingen Philologus, vols. XI, XII, XIII, XVII.

Aeneidea, or Critical, Exegetical, and Aesthetical Remarks on the Aeneis, with a personal collation of all the first class MSS., upwards of one hundred second class MSS., and all the principal editions. Vol. I, in three parts (London and Edinburgh, 1873; Dublin, 1877; Dublin, 1877). Vol. II, in three parts (Dublin, 1878; Dublin, 1879; Dublin, 1879). Vol. III, in three parts (Dublin, 1881; Dublin, 1882; Dublin 1889). Vol. IV (Dublin, 1889). Vol. V (Dublin, 1892)

Prose

A Letter to the Members of the Temperance Society, showing that the use of tea and coffee cannot be safely substituted for that of spirituous liquors, and proposing a rule of diet from which those substances are excluded (Dublin, 1830)

Letter of the Right Rev. Dr Doyce, R.C. Bishop of Kildare and Leighlin, to the Rev. George Carr, on Temperance Societies, with the Answer of James Henry, M.D. Reprinted from the Dublin Evening Post of January 2nd, and January 16th, 1830 (Dublin, 1830)

Miliaria accuratius descripta [M.D. thesis] (Dublin, 1832)

A Dialogue between a Bilious Patient and a Physician (Dublin, 1838)

An Account of the Proceedings of the Government Metropolitan Police in the City of Canton (Dublin, 1840)

An Account of the Drunken Sea (Dublin, 1840)

A Letter to the Secretaries of the Dublin Mendicity Institution. Reprinted from the Dublin Evening Post of January 20th, 1831 (Dublin, 1840)

Little Island and Big Island (Dublin, 1841)

Report of a Meeting of the Informers of Dublin held on the Sunday evening, Feb. 6th, 1842, being the day after the execution of John Delahunt for the murder of the boy Thomas Maguire (Dublin, 1842)

A Word about War (Dublin, 1842)

A Word about Judgment (Dublin, 1842)

The Unripe Windfalls of James Henry: [II] Criticism on the Style of Lord Byron, in a Letter to the Editor of "Notes and Queries" (Dublin, 1851)

Dialogue between a Stethoscopist and an Unborn Child [with *A Half Year's Poems*] (Dresden, 1854)

Cain, a Soliloquy [with *Poems Chiefly Philosophical*] (Dresden, 1856)

Religion, Wordly-Mindedness [sic] and Philosophy, being Strictures on the Autobiography of the late John Cheyne M.D., and on his Essays on Partial Derangement of the Mind in Supposed Connexion with Religion. By a Physician (Dresden, 1860)

British Legations, a letter to the Editor of the Morning Herald, concerning the late aggression on the British Embassy in Japan. By a British Subject Travelling with Her Majesty's Passport (Dresden, 1861)

The Late Yelverton Case. Letter from an Irish Protestant Conservative in Naples to his correspondent in Dublin. By 'You Know Who' (Naples, 1861). This pamphlet is attributed to Henry by John Richmond, who notes that J.S.Starkey found a copy bound in one of Henry's volumes of *Miscellanies*; Henry did not include it in his lists of publications, but this may have been because the Yelverton case was *sub judice*.

On James Henry

'James Henry', entry by W.W. [Warwick Wroth] in *Dictionary of National Biography. The New Dictionary of National Biography*, promised for 2004, will include a new entry on Henry.

John Richmond, *James Henry of Dublin: Physician, Versifier, Pamphleteer, Wanderer, and Classical Scholar* (Dublin, 1976, 64 pages). [Notable for its detailed maps of Henry's travels in relation to Virgilian holdings, and for its judgment of the classical scholarship.]

J.B.Lyons, *Scholar and Sceptic: The Career of James Henry, M.D. 1798-1876* (Dublin, 1985, 88 pages). [Notable for its illumination of Henry's medical publications and career, and for quoting extensively from his poetry and prose.]

John Richmond, "A Dedicated Life: Ireland's greatest Virgilian" (*Classics Ireland*, 1999)

from
The Unripe Windfalls
in Prose and Verse of James Henry
(1851)

Progress

YES; I'll believe in progress when I see you
Battering old jails down, and not building new;
When I behold you make but a beginning
To sleep with open doors and unbarred windows;
When I observe a thinning, not an increase,
Of your policemen and constabulary,
Your justices, and coroners, and detectives,
Your poor-law guardians and commissioners;
Grass growing in your law courts, and fell spiders
There laying snares for flies, not men for men;
And stamped receipts, recognizances, writs,
A tale of the old, Pagan, iron time,
Not of this charitable, Christian present.

I'll then believe in Progress when I hear
That fathers feel the blood mount to their cheeks,
What time they cringe, and bow, and lick the shoes
Even of the vilest clerk in the War-office,
For leave to put a motley livery suit
Upon their sons, and send them out as hirelings,
With gay cockade, and dangling sword at side,
To kill and rob and extirpate, where'er
Killing and robbing and extirpating
Opens a wider field to British commerce.

Aye; talk to me of Progress when you show me
Your city banker, or East India merchant,
After his forty years of counting-house,
And labor fruitless of all else but gold,

His bags chokeful and bursting with the weight
Of bills, and bonds, and mortgages, and scrip:
Show me, I say, your wealthy London merchant
Content with his full bags, and not intent
To cram with the like stuff still one bag more;
And come and tell me ye are making progress.

Let me observe in a full railway carriage
Some half a dozen, aye, some three, some two,
Some single solitary one that does not,
Even in the matter of front seat or back,
Or pulling up or letting down a window,
Exhibit his inveterate, ingrained,
And worse than Pharasaic, selfishness;
And I'll begin to think ye are making progress.

Here am I ready to believe in Progress
First time I hear your little girls cry "Shame!
"A coward's shame!" upon the wretch that hunts,
With horse, and hound, and cries of savage joy,
For sport, mere sport, and not to appease his hunger,
The poor, weak, timid, quivering hare to death;
And twice a coward's and an idler's shame
On him that skulks, hours, days, beside a brook,
Putting forth all the treachery and cunning
That lurk within the dark den of man's brain,
To entrap the silly troutling, and infix
Deep in his writhing gills the sly, barbed hook.
That ye are making progress I'll believe
The first time I perceive your conscience twinge ye,
For answering your questioning child with lies,
Or chill evasion of the longed-for truth;

Denying him the advantage of that knowledge
Ye purchased for yourselves with many a heartache,
And many an agony and bloody sweat;
And sending him to sail the wide, wide world,
As helpless, ignorant, and unprotected,
On board no compass, no pole-star on high,
As by your parents ye were sent yourselves,
To swim, if quick to learn; to sink, if not.

First time I hear ye say that your devotion
Has not a tide more regular than the sea,
And seldom is exactly at the full,
Just as the parish clock strikes twelve on Sunday;
And that ye count it rank hypocrisy
To go to church, and there, with heart lukewarm
Or cold, and damped with worldly cares and business,
Kneel before God, and make pretence of prayer,
In order that your children, friends, and neighbours,
May have the benefit of your good example:
That moment I'll believe ye are making progress.

When ye no longer backward start with horror
At sight of gentle Death, and wring your hands,
And weep, and cry that ye will not go with him,
Though only he can lead you to your heaven:
Then, then indeed, I'll say ye have made some progress.

from
My Book
(1853)

I KNOW not whether it be strength or weakness,
But oft, toward evening, when all round is still,
And when that day my mind has not been stirred
By any of the unholier gusts of passion,
I feel myself in the immediate presence
Of something awful, yet most fair and lovely,
And very dear, that, without sign, or action,
Or speech, communicating freely with me,
Infuses a sweet peace into my soul,
And fills it with a sentiment of joy
And happiness, that last till, from without,
Some sound alarms me, and I start, and find
The picture of my dead Love in my hand:
And they that have to do with me, those evenings,
Observe, for some hours after, in my face,
And voice, and manner, an angelic air
Of sweet content, and placid resignation.

from
A Half Year's Poems
(1854)

Pain

"PAIN, who made thee?" thus I said once
To the grim unpitying monster,
As, one sleepless night, I watched him
Heating in the fire his pincers.

"God Almighty; who dare doubt it?"
With a hideous grin he answered:
"I'm his eldest best-beloved son,
Cut from my dead mother's bowels."

"Wretch, thou liest;" shocked and shuddering
To the monster I replied then;
"God is good, and kind, and gracious;
Never made a thing so ugly."

"Tell me then, since thou know'st better,
Whose I am, by whom begotten;"
"Hell's thy birth-place, and the Devil
Both thy father and thy mother."

"Be it so; to me the same 'tis
Whether I'm God's son or grandson,
And to thee not great the difference
Once thy flesh between my tongs is."

"Spare me, spare me, Pain;" I shrieked out,
As the red-hot pincers caught me;
"Thou art God's son; aye thou'rt God's self;
Only take thy fingers off me."

"DOCTOR, when will you at home be?"
Death, one morning, thus said to me,
As I met him at a patient's—
Death and I are old acquaintance—

"I've been thinking to call on you,
But don't wish to interrupt you
In your pleasure or your business;
Say the hour that's most convenient."

"As you're so good, Death," I answered,
"Every hour to me the same is;
A friend's visit's always welcome,
Sunday, weekday, night or morning.

"But if I might make so free, Death,
I'd just beg one favor of you;
Drop in on me unexpected,
I hate ceremonious visits.

"Come to me as friend to friend comes,
On a sudden, when least thought of;
Pipes and grog are always ready,
And the matches on the table.

"Drinking, smoking, we will sit, Death,
Tête-à-tête till we grow hearty;
Then for any spree you like best,
Out we'll sally on the batter."

IT is indeed a noble sight, this hall
With its full stream of people pouring in,
Uninterrupted, at one end, and out
Uninterrupted pouring at the other.
I wish they did not disappear so soon,
That I might make acquaintance with them, learn
Something about them; whence they come, and whither
In such vast multitudes they can be going;
New faces and new faces still, and still
New faces; and beyond the faces, nothing;
Nothing beyond; black darkness fills the portal:
Out of the darkness comes the stream of faces,
Varied and fair and ever-varying faces:
I'd love them if I knew them, and if only
They did not so soon at the far door vanish
Away into impenetrable darkness,
For out beyond that portal too I see
Nothing but darkness, blank nonentity.
That incorporeal darkness has for me too
A force attractive, and toward the far portal,
Were 't but permitted, I'd go with the stream,
And for a light and airy Negative
Exchange this Positive's too oppressive weight.

Man's Universal Hymn

THE Lord's my God and still shall be,
For a kind God he is to me,
And gives me a carte-blanche to rob
His other creatures, and to fob
For my own use their property,
So good and kind he is to me.
He bids me pluck the goose and take
Her soft warm down my bed to make,
Then turn her out with raw skin bare
To shiver in the cold, night air;
Her new-laid eggs he bids me steal
To make me a delicious meal,
And, when she has no more to lay,
Commands me cram her every day
With oaten meal 'till she's so plump
The fat's an inch deep on her rump,
Then cut her throat and roast and eat,
And thank him for the luscious treat.

The Lord's my God and still shall be,
For a kind God he is to me;
He makes the bee construct his cell
Of yellow wax and fill it well
With honey for his winter store,
And, when it's so full 'twill hold no more,
Comes and points out the hive to me,
And says:—"I give it all to thee;
Small need 's for winter store the bee
Who never a winter is to see;

Kill him and eat his honey thou,
I'm the bee's God, and thee allow."

I love the Lord my God, for he
Loves all his creatures tenderly,
But more than all his creatures, me.
He bids me from the dam's side tear
The tender lambkin and not spare:—
"Piteous though bleat the orphan'd dam,
Turn a deaf ear and dine on lamb."

I love the Lord my God, for he
Loves all his creatures tenderly,
But more than all his creatures, me.
He bids the gallant horse live free
And more than life love liberty;
Then says to me:—"The horse is thine;
Thou shalt in slavery make him pine;
Confine him in a dungeon dim,
Fetter him every joint and limb,
Maim him, cut off his tail and ears—
Thou know'st the use of knife and shears—
A red-hot brand the bleeding sears;
Don't mind his quivering or his groans,
I'd have men's hearts as hard as stones.
So far so good, but much remains
Still to be done ere for thy pains
Thou hast a willing, servile brute,
Who shall not dare the will dispute
Of his taskmaster; a bold, free
And noble spirit he has from me,
And worse than death hates slavery;
This noble spirit how to quell

I'll teach thee now—remember well
I am the God and friend of both
The horse and thee, and would be loth
Either to one or to the other
Aught ill should happen; thou'st a brother
In every creature great or small;
The same Lord God has made ye all—
So when thou'st cropped him ears and tail,
And maimed him so he's neither male
Nor female more, fasten a strong
Stout bar of iron with a thong
Between his jaws; then through a ring
In the bar's near end run a string
Of twisted hemp, and hold it tight
In thy left hand, while with thy right
Thou scourgest him with a long lash so
That, will-he nill-he, he must go—
Not onward, for thou hast him bound
Fast by the jaw, but round and round,
Thou in the middle standing still
And plying the lash with right good will;
At first, no doubt, he'll fume and fret
And fall perhaps into a sweat
Of agony, and upward rear,
And spurn the ground, and paw the air—
What is't to thee? lash thou the more;
When tired behind, begin before,
Still holding him by the muzzle fast;
Pain breaks the stoutest heart at last;
Ere a short month he'll do thy will,
Gallop, trot, canter or stand still
At thy least bidding, carry, draw,
And labour for thee until raw

And galled his flesh and blind his eyes
And lame his feet, and so he dies,
If thou so little know'st of thrift
And of the right use of my gift
Of all my creatures unto thee
Both great and small whate'er they be,
As to allow thine old worn-out
And battered slave to go about
Consuming good food every day
And standing awkward in the way,
When for the fee of his shoes and hide
Thou might'st have all his wants supplied
By the knacker's knife; be merciful
And when he can no longer pull,
Nor carry thee upon his back,
To the knacker send thy hack."

Ye little birds, in God rejoice,
And praise him with melodious voice:
Small though ye are, he minds ye all,
And "never to the ground shall fall
A sparrow without his consent,"
By which beyond all doubt is meant—
Man, take thy victim; clip his wing;
Put out his eyes that he may sing
As sweet in winter as in spring;
Confine him in close prison-house
Where scarcely could turn round a mouse;
What though I made him wild and free
In the wood to range from tree to tree
And more than life love liberty,
Let it not fret thee, he is thine
By virtue of a writ divine—

Cage him, if he sings soft and sweet;
If bad his voice, kill him and eat.

Indwellers of the deep, blue sea,
To praise the Lord unite with me;
Ye grampuses and mighty whales
That lash the water with your tails
Into a foam, and spirt it high
Up through your nostrils to the sky,
Rejoice with me; the Lord of heaven
Into my hands your lives has given,
And taught me how best to pursue
And hunt ye through the waters blue
With barbed harpoon, till far and wide
The ocean with your life's blood's dyed.

Ye salmon, herring, wide-mouthed cod,
Praise in your hearts the Lord your God,
Who has made you of the ocean free,
Then whispered in the ear to me:—
"Go, take thy nets and trawl for fish;
On fast-days they're an excellent dish
With vinegar, mustard and cayenne"—
Praise ye the Lord; I'll say Amen.

Come hither, every living thing,
And in full chorus with me sing
The praise of him who reigns above,
The God of justice, and of love,
Who for my use has made ye all,
Bird, beast, fish, insect; great and small.
For me ye build, for me ye breed;

For me ye work, for me ye bleed;
I fatten on ye; ye are mine;
Come praise with me the work divine
And its great author, just and good,
Who has given ye all to me for food,
Clothing or pleasure, or mere sport;
His praise to all the ends report
Of the wide earth: sing, ever sing,
The all-righteous maker, father, king.

Contempt of Court

HE* sat upon the judgment-seat in ermine,
And judged the causes as they came before him;
Heard counsel plead, and weighed the evidence
On both sides to a hair; then charged the jury,
Expounding to them statute, law, and custom,
And laid the case before them disembarrassed
Of all its ambiguity and clear
And palpable to every comprehension;
Then took their verdict and pronounced his fiat,
Which his apparitors contended who
Would first and speediest put in execution.
While he was thus engaged came Finis, sudden,
And, in direct contempt of Court, a smart tap
With his forefinger struck him on the forehead,
And down he fell, his ermine discomposing,
And left the unfinished sentence and the crowds
That waited on his words as on a God's;
And three or four men came and in their arms
Carried away a foul, disgusting carcase.

*"At the opening of the Commission here this morning for the trial of
prisoners, Mr. Justice Talfourd was seized with an apoplectic fit while
charging the Jury, and expired in less than five minutes". *Stafford Journal*,
March 13, 1854.

Out of the Frying Pan into the Fire

I DREAMT one night—it was a horrid dream—
That I was dead, and made was the division
Between the innocent flesh and guilty spirit,
And that the former, with a white sheet wrapt round
And nailed up in a box, was to the bottom
Sunk of a deep and narrow pit, which straight
Was filled to overheaping with a mixture
Of damp clay, rotting flesh and mouldering bones,
And lidded with a weighty stone whereon
Was writ my name and on what days precise
I first and last drew breath; while up the latter
Flew, without help of wings or fins or members,
By its mere lightness, through the air, to heaven;
And there being placed before the judgment-seat
Of its Maker, and most unsatisfactory
Answer returning to the question:—"Wherefore
Wast thou as I made thee?" was sent down
Tumbling by its own weight, down down to Hell,
To sink or swim or wade as best it might,
In sulphurous fires unquenchable for ever,
With Socrates and Plato, Aristides
Falsely surnamed the just, and Zoroaster,
Titus the good, and Cato and divine
Homer and Virgil, and so many millions
And millions more of wrongfully called good
And wise and virtuous, that for want of sulphur
And fire and snakes and instruments of torture
And room in Hell, the Universal Maker
Was by his own inherent justice forced,
That guilt might not go scot-free and unpunished,

To set apart so large a share of Heaven
For penal colonies and jails and treadmills,
That mutinies for want of flying-space
Began t' arise among the cherubim
And blessed spirits, and a Proclamation
Of Martial Law in Heaven was just being read
When, in a sweat of agony and fear,
I woke, and found myself in Germany,
In the close prison of a German bed,
And at my bedside Mr. Oberkellner
With printed list of questions in his hand:
My name and age and birthplace and religion,
Trade or profession, wherefore I had come,
How long to stay, whither next bound, and so forth;
All at my peril to be truly answered,
And upon each a sixpence to the State,
Which duly paid I should obtain permission
To stay where I was so long as the State pleased,
Without being prosecuted as a felon,
Spy, or disturber of the public peace.

DEATH, I'd beg one favor of thee:
Whensoe'er thou'rt pleased to take me
From my weeping Katharine, take me
All at once—I'd have no Farewells
Where the parting is for ever.

My Stearine Candles

HE'S gone to bed at last, that flaring, glaring,
Round, red-faced, bold, monopolizing Sun,
And I may venture from their hiding-place
To bring my pair of stearine candles forth
And set them, firmly stayed, upon my table,
To illuminate and cheer my studious evening.
Thou hast my praise, Prometheus, for thy theft,
And, were I to idolatry addicted,
Shouldst be my God in preference to Buddh,
Brahma, or Thor, or Odin, or Jove's self.
Her of the olive branch I'd hold to thee
The next in honor, and before her shrine
In gratitude would keep for ever burning
A lamp of such Athenian oil as Plato,
Demosthenes, Pythagoras, and Solon
Were wont in bed to read by, after midnight.
The third, last person of my Trinity
Should be th' inventor of the stearine candle;
He that enabled me to sit, the long
Midwinter nights, in study, by a light
Which neither flickers nor offends the nostrils,
Nor from the distance of a thousand miles,
Or thousand years, or both perhaps, keeps ever
And anon calling me—like some bold child
The mother's hand—to come and snuff and snub it;
But steady, cleanly, bright and inodorous,
Than tallow more humane, than wax less costly,
Gives me just what I want, and asks back nothing.

BUDDHA, the humane and kindly,
As he travelled through a jungle,
Came to where lay stretched a tigress
With her four cubs, weak and hungry.

Buddha with him you may guess well
No food had to suit a tigress,
And the nearest house was miles off,
And the tigress' case was urgent.

What hadst thou done, gentle reader,
Hadst thou been in his position?
Ah! I doubt not, left the tigress
With her cubs to die of hunger.

Or hadst thou the necessary
Courage had, and murderous weapons,
Thou hadst slain and out of pain put
Both the tigress and her four cubs.

But a different heart was Buddha's,
And his false religion taught him
Sympathy with all things living,
And to do good, to his own loss.

And he'd always been accustomed
To think humbly of his own self,
And did not believe God's creatures
Were made solely to be man's slaves.

So he went, and not with Christian
Verbal self-humiliation,
But in fact himself despising,
And his fellow creature pitying,

Laid himself beside the tigress
And her four cubs, for their supper—
All in vain! they're too exhausted
To lay fang or claw upon him.

Get up, Buddha, and be off fast;
Thou hast done enough in conscience;
Curtius, Regulus and the Decii
Are but egotists beside thee.

Different Buddha's way of thinking:
From the ground he picks a sharp stone,
Cuts his finger and the blood smears
On the tigress's and cubs' lips.

Never to tired pilgrim's parched mouth
Drop of wine half so refreshing,
As the taste of Buddha's warm blood
To the famished cubs and tigress.

First they licked their lips, their ears cocked,
And from sleep seemed as if waking,
Languidly on Buddha's head then
Laid one of the cubs his forepaws.

Buddha's pity 's not away thrown;
Taste of blood 's elixir vitae
For your Bluecoat and your Redcoat,
Why not for your jungle tigress?

With returning strength and fierceness
Fell the tigress and her four cubs
On the meal by Providence sent them,
And no bone left of kind Buddha.

Ο ΠΟΙΗΤΗΣ

IN my well bolstered study chair as once
In busy idleness I sat, reflecting
On human vanity, there came a thought
With such a lively motion 'cross my brain,
That from my seat I started and cried out,
Though there was no one within call or hearing:—
"I'll do it and begin this very moment.
What though I'm inexperienced, and before
Have never anything of a similar kind
Attempted, there's a charm in novelty
That recompenses labor, failure, blunders;
Better and nobler even the abortive effort
Than sheer do-nothing, mere passivity,
Dull vegetation in my elbow chair."
So saying I rang the bell, and bade my servant
Bring me a billet of wood out of the cellar,
And a sharp knife, back-saw, and whetting stone,
Oil and a chisel, and should any one
Ask for me, enjoined him strictly he should answer
That I was sick, busy, or dead, and could not,
Would not, and at the peril of his place
Should not be interrupted:—"For I was"—
But here my prudence interposing cried:—
"Silence!" and with my hand I motioned him
Out of the room, and straightway fell to work.
And, first, of all the unsightly prominences
And residue of bark I cleared the billet,
And, having satisfied myself that sound

[title: *the poet*]

And suited for my purpose was the wood,
Drew with the point of my knife a circle round it,
Nearer so much to one end than the other,
That one end for the head, the other end
Might for the trunk serve and extremities
Of the doll whose image, sketch or prototype
Had for some days, weeks, months past, like a ghost,
Haunted me day and night, sleeping and waking.
The circle then with my knife's edge I notched,
Deepened and widened, and by slow degrees
Fashioned into a neck not utterly
Inelegant or shapeless; next the corners
So pared and rounded of the shorter end,
That underneath my diligent hand I soon
Began to see a head growing apace,
With nose, ears, cheekbones, brow, and underjaw,
And on the skull sufficient prominences,
Moral and intellectual, to fill
The heart of a phrenologist with rapture.
A transverse slit the mouth made, and for sockets
The eyes had two holes burnt out with the red hot
Point of an old, attenuated poker;
Two kidney-beans, stripped of their shells and rounded,
Did very well for eyeballs, and had each
A pupil in a jet-black miniature wafer.
The seat of reason and expression thus
Completed happily, I had less care
About the more ignoble parts; a few
Bold, rough and rapid strokes turned all below
The neck into the taper trunk of a Hermes;
Inscribed on which with eager, trembling hand
ΑΥΤΟΣ ΕΠΟΙΕΙ and the poet's name,
[*he was making it, doing it*]

I sat me down to admire and contemplate
My handywork, and had perhaps till now
Continued sitting, and admiring still,
Had not a gentle tap come to the door,
And, peeping in, my servant:—"Please, Sir—morning;
And breakfast more than two hours on the table."

Dialogue between a Stethoscopist
and an Unborn Child
(1854)

Dialogue between a Stethoscopist and an Unborn Child

STETHESCOPIST *(applying the Stethoscope)*. Holla! any one there?

CHILD *(within)*. Who calls?

S. A friend.

C. Let me alone; what do you want?

S. The time's come; all's ready.

C. What time's come? what's all ready?

S. Warm water, clothes, and nurse.

C. What warm water? what clothes? what nurse?

S. Warm water to wash you, clothes to dress you, nurse to suckle you.

C. Don't want any of them—wont have any of them.

S. You must have them; you can't do without them.

C. I can, and I will; let me alone.

S. I wont let you alone, you must come—you must have them.

C. I say I wont. Who are you at all? or what have you to do with me?

S. I'm the Doctor.

C. Who's the Doctor? what's the Doctor for?

S. To take care of you—to do you good.

C. I don't want any care; I don't want any good. I'm well enough as I am.

S. Come; you shall and must.

C. I wont; where do you want me to go? what do you want me to do? let me alone.

S. I want you to come here—to come to me.

C. Where are you?

S. Here.

C. Where?

S. Here.

C. Where's here?

S. Here.

C. Go away; let me alone.

S. Come, I say.

C. I wont.

S. You must.

C. You'll do something to me if I go.

S. Never mind, but come.

C. Tell me first will anything be done to me if I go.

S. Yes, you'll be washed.

C. What'll I be washed for?

S. To make you clean.

C. I'm clean enough—let me alone. If I go, is that all will be done to me?

S. No; after you're washed you'll be dressed—the clothes will be put on you.

C. What for?

S. To keep the cold from you.

C. Then it's cold where you are?

S. Yes.

C. I wont go.

S. You must.

C. I wont go where it's cold.

S. You wont feel the cold once the clothes are on you.

C. Well, is that all? will it do when I've got the clothes on me?

S. No, you must get suck.

C. What's suck for?

S. To keep you from growing sick, and dying.

C. What's growing sick, and dying?

S. You can't understand that yet.

C. Well then, when I'm washed and get on the clothes, and take the suck, is that all?

S. No; that's only the beginning; after that you must get medicine.

C. What's that?

S. Something to keep you from growing sick, and dying.

C. Then it's the same as suck?

S. Not quite, but for the same purpose.

C. I wont go. It's a bad place you're in.

S. Good or bad, you must come.

C. Well, is there any thing else after the medicine, or is it the last?

S. Then the clothes are to be taken off you, and you are to be washed again.

C. And that's all?

S. No; then the clothes will be put on you again, and you'll get suck again, and then—

C. I tell you I won't go at all; let me alone; I wont talk to you any more.

S. Make haste.

No answer.

S. Make haste, I say.

No answer.

S. Holla! holla!

C. Let me alone; go out of that.

S. Are you coming?

C. No; would you have me go to where it's cold, and where I must be washed twice, and put on clothes twice, and take suck twice, and medicine twice?

S. Like it or not it's all one—come you must.

C. Well if you promise me that I'll have to do all you say only twice—

S. I'll make no promises—I'd be sorry to deceive you.

C. Must I do it all more than twice?

S. Yes; very often—over and over again.

C. How often?

S. I don't know; very, very often. You'll be always doing some one or other of these things, or having some one or other of these things done to you, or if not exactly one of these things, something pretty much the same.

C. How often in all do you think?

S. I really can't say how often; almost always until you die.

C. Die! I thought you said doing these things would keep me from dying.

S. Yes, for a little while, but not always.

C. How long?

S. I really can't say. You will die immediately if you don't do them; and not quite so soon if you do.

C. Then if I go, I think I wont do them at all. Better die a little sooner and save all the trouble.

S. You would not say that, if you knew what a terrible thing death is.

C. Go away; it's very bad of you to want me to go to a place where there must be always something doing to me to keep me from dying, and where nothing will keep me long from it. I wonder you would ask me to go to such a place at all.

S. Staying where you are wont save you; you'll die equally whether you stay there or come here.

C. Then I'll stay here, where there's nothing to be done to me, rather than go to you where there's so much to be done to me to so little purpose.

S. But it makes a great difference whether you die where you are or here.

C. Why, what difference does it make? Didn't you say it was a terrible thing to die where you are? what worse can it be to die here?

S. A great deal worse—no comparison worse.

C. How's that? I don't understand that; it's dying in both cases; where you are, after much trouble and doing all manner of things to keep yourself from dying, and here, after no trouble at all.

S. Poor innocent child, how little you know about it! I pity you.

C. Do you know I think I'd begin to like you if you wouldn't frighten me so. I'd never have known any thing about dying if you hadn't told me—but what's the difference between dying here and where you are? it's dying, after all.

S. The difference is this: if you die where you are, you'll remain dead for ever; if you die here, you'll be made alive again, and never die any more.

C. Then my mind's made up to staying and dying here. Alive, and dead, and then alive again, seems to me a very clumsy round-about way; once dead, I think one may as well remain dead, and no more about it; especially if the life one is to have after being made alive again, is anything like the life you say you have where you are.

S. I shudder when I hear you talk so. It is an awful thing to die and remain dead for ever.

C. As to the dying, you have it equally whether you remain dead or are made alive again; and as to the remaining dead, who knows but if I were made alive again I would come in for as bad a life as you say you have where you are.

S. It would be either a great deal better or a great deal worse than this; certainly not the same—not like this at all.

C. Would it be like what I have here?

S. No, not at all—quite different.

C. Then how do I know that I would like it?

S. If you happened upon the one that is worse than this, you certainly would not like it, for it is made on purpose that you should not; but if you happened upon the other, it is equally certain that you would like it, for it is made on purpose that you should.

C. And which would I be most likely to happen on?

S. Why, to tell you the truth, you would be beyond all comparison most likely to happen on the one you wouldn't like.

C. What are the odds?

S. I don't know precisely; some say a thousand to one, some say a hundred thousand to one, some a million to one.

C. I believe you take me for a fool.

S. Why?

C. To suppose I would think for a minute of running such a chance. But stay— would I be let come back again if I didn't like that second life?

S. No; never.

C. And I must always stay in it no matter how much I disliked it?

S. Yes; for ever and ever and ever without end.

C. And do you really think me such a fool? No; if I must die I'll stay and die here, where I am sure of not being made alive again. I'll run none of your chances.

S. By doing so you lose all chance; not only the chance of the bad life, but the chance of the good one also.

C. How do I know I would like the good life, as you call it, even if I was so lucky as to get it? maybe I mightn't think it good at all; and even if I should find it as good as you say, I wouldn't like to go and live where you are, in order to get it; it is a shocking idea to me, to go where I must be always washing, and putting on and off clothes, and taking suck and medicine, and then, after all, dying, and being made alive again with nine hundred and ninety nine chances in a thousand that I would get a life made purposely to be disagreeable to me and in which I must stay and live for ever, and only one chance in a thousand of my getting a life intended to be agreeable to me, and if I should be so fortunate as to hit upon that thousandth or hundred thousandth or millionth chance, finding after all that it was the very kind of life that above all others I hated.

S. I say again you don't know what an awful thing it is to remain dead for ever.

C. How do you know better than I? Were you ever dead for ever?

S. No; certainly not.

C. Then how do you know it's such a terrible thing?

S. Why really I don't know from experience, but I guess it is so.

C. Then it's nothing but a guess you're making all this work about. Can you tell me what being dead for ever and never made alive again is like?

S. No, I cannot.

C. And yet it's so awful? It's being made alive again should be awful to you, and not being let remain dead.

S. Why?

C. Because the second life must be at least something like the first else it wouldn't be life at all, and the first according to your own account of it is awful enough.

S. I have just thought of something that being dead for ever is like.

C. Well, let's hear.

S. Why, I should think it's very like the state we were in during the past Ever.

C. What state's that?

S. The state of not being at all—the state of nothing, or nothingness.

C. Well, at all events there's nothing bad in nothing—neither good nor bad; it's sheer nothing, and therefore neither bad nor awful.

S. I see there's no use in arguing with you.

C. Not a bit, unless you argue better than you have done yet. Every word you have said has only made me more determined to stay where I am.

S. I wanted to persuade you to agree to what you couldn't help—to do willingly what you must do whether you will or no.

C. You have just produced the opposite effect.

S. Well, I must say I rejoice that it does not depend on your will; that you will be forced to your good.

C. It's a sad condition to be forced to do what you think good, and I think bad. Would you like to be forced to do what I think good, and you think bad?

S. No matter whether I would like it or not, it's the very condition in which you are.

C. Alas! Alas! what a sad condition! well at all events I'll stay here till I'm forced.

S. If you only knew what a fine thing is to happen to you on the road, you'd be in a hurry to come at once—you'd think you never could be here soon enough.

C. Hah! hah! hah!

S. What makes you laugh?

C. I'm laughing at yourself. When you find you can't frighten me into what you want, you think you'll try what coaxing and cajoling will do. Go on; what fine thing's to happen me?

S. On the way between where you are and where I am, you're to get a soul.

C. A soul! what's that?

S. I can't describe it to you better than by saying it's a soul, a spirit.

C. At least you can tell me what it's like.

S. No, I can't.

C. Did you ever see one?

S. No, I never did.

C. Did you ever feel one?

S. No, never.

C. Ever taste, or smell, or hear one?

S. No.

C. Have you one yourself?

S. Yes.

C. Have you it long?

S. Yes; as long as I can remember.

C. Then surely you must have either seen or felt or tasted or smelled or heard it before this.

S. No.

C. Then how do you know you have it?

No answer.

C. What use is it to you?

73

No answer.

C. Where did you get it?

S. On the way between where you are and where I am.

C. Then you were once here?

S. Not exactly there, but in a precisely similar place.

C. And were forced out of it as I am to be forced out of this?

S. Yes.

C. And got the soul on the way?

S. Yes.

C. Whereabouts on the way did you get it?

S. I don't know.

C. Was it near here or near there?

S. I don't know.

C. Was it waiting for you, or was it coming to meet you?

S. I don't know.

C. Where was it before you got it?

S. I don't know.

C. What did you do with it when you got it?

S. Nothing.

C. But you're quite sure you got it?

S. Yes, perfectly sure.

C. And have it still?

S. Yes.

C. Where?

S. I don't know.

C. Was there warm water and clothes and suck and medicine waiting for you too?

S. Yes.

C. Maybe the soul was in some of them.

S. No; I got it first.

C. Between the place you were forced out of, and the first washing?

S. Yes.

C. Was it far between?

S. No, quite close.

C. That was lucky; you hadn't to go far looking about for it.

S. No; I hadn't to look for it; I didn't know anything about it at all.

C. Then nobody had told you about it, as you have told me?

S. No; I was forced out at once without any notice.

C. My obligation to you's the greater.

S. I beg you'll not mention it.

C. It's well you got it at all, as you weren't expecting it, didn't know anything about it, and couldn't either have seen or felt it, if you had; I suppose it knew about you.

S. I think it must, else how so exactly hit the nick of time?

C. Wouldn't it have done equally well a little later—suppose after your first being washed and dressed and getting suck and medicine?

S. No; not by any means as well.

C. Why?

S. I might have died in the interval, and then what would have become of me?

C. You needn't ask me; it's I should ask you; tell me what would have become of you in that case.

S. I should have remained dead for ever.

C. Now I begin to understand you; it's by means of this soul you get the second life. Am I right?

S. Perfectly; the soul is immortal, never dies.

C. Then the soul has only one life; what never dies can't have two lives, unless it has them both together.

S. Certainly.

C. But you die, don't you?

S. Yes, to be sure.

C. And are made alive again?

S. Yes.

C. Then while you're dead what becomes of the soul that never dies?

S. I never thought of that.

C. Well, no matter about that; I suppose it will be taken care of, as it was before you got it.

S. I have no doubt of it.

C. It will be kept for you and you'll get it again when you're made alive the second time, just as you got it when you were made alive the first time?

S. I suppose so; there can indeed be no doubt of it.

C. Then after all it's not by means of the soul you get the second life, any more than it's by means of the soul you get the first life; on the contrary you get the soul after you have already got the second life, just as you get the soul after you have already got the first life. If I'm not right I hope you'll correct me.

S. You must be right, for it's certain I die, and it's equally certain the soul never dies.

C. Then the way is really this: First you're made alive, as I am now, without any soul; then you go from where I am to where you are, and on the way you get the soul; then you die, and, as the soul never dies, it leaves you and you are without a soul again; then you are made alive again, and then finally you get the soul again.

S. Just so; I think that is a very clear account of the matter.

C. You're made alive first each time, and get the soul after; and the first time you get the soul it doesn't hinder you from dying, but the second time it does.

S. Yes.

C. It's a pity it hasn't the virtue the first time you get it.

S. Aye, that it is! then we'd have no dying at all; that indeed would be the fine thing!

C. I don't mean that it would be better there should be no dying—unless indeed one would be allowed to stay always where I am at present—but as you tell me that can't be, and that I must go to where you are whether I like it or not, then I think it's better there should be dying, provided only that dying was final and would put an end to your trouble; but as you inform me again that it's not final and will not put an end to your trouble, but rather be the beginning of it, and that after being dead for a while, you are to be made alive again, and live on for ever, just as if you had never been dead, then I think it better to have no dying, at all, for what is it but mere lost trouble—sheer bad management—bother for nothing?—Stay, what's that pulling me? Is that the soul? am I getting the soul now?

S. As there's no use in talking to you—

C. Oh! oh! oh! don't pull me so hard.

S. Come along—this way—come along—

C. Oh! oh! oh!

S. Come along, I say—come along, my little philosopher—come along—

from
Poems Chiefly Philosophical
(1856)

Old Man

AT six years old I had before mine eyes
A picture painted, like the rainbow, bright,
But far, far off in th' unapproachable distance.
With all my childish heart I longed to reach it,
And strove and strove the livelong day in vain,
Advancing with slow step some few short yards
But not perceptibly the distance lessening.
At threescore years old, when almost within
Grasp of my outstretched arms the selfsame picture
With all its beauteous colors painted bright,
I'm backward from it further borne each day
By an invisible, compulsive force,
Gradual but yet so steady, sure, and rapid,
That at threescore and ten I'll from the picture
Be even more distant than I was at six.

Very Old Man

I WELL remember how some threescore years
And ten ago, a helpless babe, I toddled
From chair to chair about my mother's chamber,
Feeling, as 'twere, my way in the new world
And foolishly afraid of, or, as 't might be,
Foolishly pleased with, th' unknown objects round me.
And now with stiffened joints I sit all day
In one of those same chairs, as foolishly
Hoping or fearing something from me hid
Behind the thick, dark veil which I see hourly
And minutely on every side round closing
And from my view all objects shutting out.

SWEET breathes the hawthorn in the early spring
And wallflower petals precious fragrance fling,
Sweet in July blows full the cabbage rose
And in rich beds the gay carnation glows,
Sweet smells on sunny slopes the new-mown hay,
And belle-de-nuit smells sweet at close of day,
Sweet under southern skies the orange bloom
And lank acacia spread their mild perfume,
But of all odorous sweets I crown thee queen,
Plain, rustic, unpretending, black eyed bean.

Heaven

"SO this is Heaven," said I to my conductor,
"And I'm at last in full and sure possession
Of life eternal; let me look about me.
Methinks, somehow, it's not what I expected;
Nor can I say I feel that full delight,
That extasy I had anticipated.
Perhaps the reason is, it's all so new,
And I must here, as on the Earth below,
Grow by degrees accustomed and inured."
My guide replied not, but went on before me,
I following:—"Are you sure we are in Heaven?"
Said I, growing uneasy; for I saw
Neither bright sky, nor sun, nor flowers, nor trees;
Heard no birds caroling, no gurgling waters;
Far less saw angel forms, heard angel voices
Singing in chorus praise to the Most High;
But all was blank and desert, dim and dull,
Misty, obscure and undistinguishable,
Formless and void as if seen through thick fog
Or not seen through, but only the fog seen,
The fog alone, monotonous, uniform,
Rayless, impenetrable, cheerless, dark;
And all was silent as beneath the ocean
Ten thousand thousand fathom, or at the centre
Of the solid Earth; and when I strove to speak
I started, started when I strove to hear
My guide's responses; for neither my guide
Nor I spoke humanly, nor in a human
Language, for I had left my tongue on Earth,
To rot with my body, and had become a spirit

Voiceless and earless, eyeless and etherial,
And with my guide, for he too was a spirit,
Conversed by consciousness without the aid
Of voice or tongue or ears or signs or sounds:—
"If this indeed is Heaven," said I at last
Or strove or wished to say, "in pity bring me
Out of the waste and horrid wilderness
To where there is some light, some sound, some voice,
Some living thing, some stir, some cheerfulness."
"Spirit, thou talk'st as thou wert still in the flesh,
And still hadst eyes to see, and ears to hear,
And touch wherewith to hold communication
With solid and material substances.
What use were light here where there are no eyes?
What use were sounds here where there are no ears?
What use were substance where there are no bodies?
Here cheerful stir or action would but harm
Where every thing's already in perfection,
Already in its right, most fitting place.
Nay, sigh not, spirit; this is thy wished Heaven."
"At least there is communion among spirits,
Spirits know and love each other, spirits hope,
Spirits rejoice together, and together
Sing Hallelujahs to the Lord their God."
"I said that spirits sing not, when I said
Spirits have neither voices, tongues, nor ears;
And where's the room for hope, or love, or knowledge
Where there's no heart, brain, ignorance or passion?
With thy conductor there's indeed communion,
Such as between us now, till thou'rt installed
And in complete possession; of itself
Then ceases all communion, useless grown;
And thou art left in thy beatitude,

Untouched, unstirred, through all eternity;
Without all care, all passion, hope and fear;
Nothing to do or suffer, seek or avoid."
"Then bring me, ere communion wholly ceases,
Quick bring me to my mother's sainted spirit.
Mainly that I might once more see my mother,
Know and embrace and to my bosom press her,
Longed I for Heaven; quick, kind conductor, quick."
"Thou hast no mother, spirit; never hadst.
Spirits engender not, nor are engendered.
She whom thou call'st thy mother, was the mother
Not of thy spiritual, but thy fleshly nature.
Thou, spirit, com'st from God, and having dwelt
Some few, brief seasons in the fleshly body
Engendered by the flesh thou call'st thy mother
Return'st, by me conducted, back to Heaven,
Leaving behind thee in the Earth to rot
The consanguineous flesh, mother and son."
"Then bring me to the spirit that sometime
Dwelt in that flesh which mixed with other flesh
The flesh engendered which, below on Earth,
So long as it lived, afforded me kind shelter."
"Thou know'st not what thou ask'st, scarce spiritual spirit;
Even were communion possible in Heaven
Twixt spirits which on Earth had grown acquainted
Through th' accident of having inhabited
Related bodies, such communion were
In this case out of the question, for the spirit
Which chanced to have its dwelling in that flesh
By which the flesh in which thou dwelt'st on Earth
Was generated, is not here in Heaven,
But down, down, down at the other side of the Earth,
Down in the depths of Hell, for ever there

Condemned by the unchangeable decree
Of the Allmerciful, to writhe in torment."
He said, or seemed to say; with horror struck
I shrieked, methought, and swooned, and know no more.

ANOTHER and another and another
And still another sunset and sunrise,
The same yet different, different yet the same,
Seen by me now in my declining years
As in my early childhood, youth and manhood;
And by my parents and my parents' parents,
And by the parents of my parents' parents,
And by their parents counted back for ever,
Seen, all their lives long, even as now by me;
And by my children and my children's children
And by the children of my children's children
And by their children counted on for ever
Still to be seen as even now seen by me;
Clear and bright sometimes, sometimes dark and clouded
But still the same sunsetting and sunrise;
The same for ever to the never ending
Line of observers, to the same observer
Through all the changes of his life the same:
Sunsetting and sunrising and sunsetting,
And then again sunrising and sunsetting,
Sunrising and sunsetting evermore.

WELL now I'm sure I don't know why in the world it was put there,
Standing up in the middle of the face like the gnomon of a sundial,
Very much, as one would say, in the way of the passers by,
And exposed to heat and cold, wet and dry, all the winds that blow.

Don't tell me that it was for the sake of beauty it was ever set up there,
Still less that it was for utility, i. e. by way of a handle,
And as to the hints I sometimes hear that it was out of mere
                              whim or vagary,
I assure you I'm not the man to lend an ear to insinuations of that sort.

But I'll tell you the idea that has just now flashed across my mind
And which of course I hold myself at liberty to correct as I
                              improve in knowledge,
For these are improving times, as you know, and the whole
                              world's in progress,
And the only wonder is, that with all our advancement we're so very
far behind yet.

Now my idea's neither more nor less than that it was set up where
                              it is simply because God
Hadn't, or couldn't at the moment find, a more convenient spot
                              to put it in;
And I'm further of opinion that if you or I had had the placing of it,
It's no better but a thousand times worse it would have been
                              placed than now it is.

For while I admit that it does indeed at first sight seem a little
                              too far forward set,
Like a camp picket or vedette upon the very fore front and edge
                              of danger,
Still there's no denying the solidity and security of its basis,
And that it rarely if ever happens it's obliged to evacuate its position.

Why, I've seen an enemy come up to it in a towering fit of passion,
And with his right hand clenched till it looked like a sledge-
                              hammer or mason's mallet
Strike it such a blow right in the face as you'd swear must annihilate it,
Or at least send its ghost down dolefully whimpering to Orcus.

Nay, I've seen its best friend and nearest earthly relative
With a giant's grasp lay hold of it, and squeeze it between finger
                              and thumb,
Till it roared with downright agony as loud as a braying ass or elephant,
And yet, the moment after, it seemed not a hair the worse but
                              rather refreshed by it.

But all this is scarce worth mentioning in comparison of what
                              I've seen it bear
At the hands of that same natural friend, ally, and protector,
Who twenty times a day or, if the humor happened so to take him,
A hundred times a day would in one of the dark cellars under it

Explode all on a sudden so strong a detonating powder
That you'd say there never yet was iron tower or vaulted
                              granite casemate
That wouldn't have tumbled down incontinent at the very first
                              concussion,
And yet that wondrous piece of flesh and bone seemed but to take
                              delight in it.

But, setting aside these wholly minor and secondary considerations,
What would you say of an architect who had constructed a face
With a pair of eyes staring, one on the right side and the other
                              on the left side of it,
And yet had made no manner of provision at all for the support
                              of a pair of spectacles?

So avaunt with your idle criticisms, your good-for-nothing stuff
                              and twaddle,
Such as one dozes over a-nights in the Quarterly just before one
                              goes to bed,
And let me have a pinch out of your canister, for I know
                              it's the genuine Lundy
More care-easing even than Nepenthe, than Ambrosia
                              more odoriferous.

Letter

Received from a reviewer to whom the author, intending to send
the MS. of his Six Photographs of the Heroic Times for review, had
by mistake sent, instead of it, a MS. of Milton's Paradise Regained.

WITH all the care and attention permitted by my multitudinous
And harassing, yet never upon any account to be neglected, avocations,
I have read over, verse by verse, from near about the beginning
      to the very end,
The poem which, some thirteen or fourteen months ago, you
      did me the honor to enclose me;
And as I feel for literature in general and especially for literary men
A regard which I make bold to flatter myself is something more
      than merely professional,
In returning you your work I venture to make these few
      hurried observations:

And first, I'm so far from being of opinion that the work's
      wholly devoid of merit
That I think I can discern here and there an odd half line or line in it,
Which even Lord Byron himself—for since Lord Byron became popular,
Reviewers' opinions concerning that truly great man have
      undergone, as you know, a most remarkable change—
I think I can discern, I say, here and there in your work an
      odd half line or odd line
Which even the greatest poet of modern times need not have
      been ashamed of.
And the whole scope and tenor of your work, on whichever
      side or in whatever light I examine it,
Whether religiously, esthetically, philosophically, morally or
      simply poetically,

Give me great ground to hope—and I assure you I feel
        unfeigned satisfaction in expressing the hope—
That, in process of time, and supposing your disposition amenable
        to advice and correction,
You may by dint of study and perseverance acquire sufficient
        poetical skill
To entitle you to a place somewhere or other among respectable
        English poets.

And now I know I may count upon your good sense and
        candor to excuse me
If I add to this, you'll do me the justice to allow, no illiberal
        praise of your performance,
Some few honest words of dispraise, wrung from me by the
        necessity of the case:
Your style, for I will not mince the matter, seems to me very often to be
A little too Bombastes Furioso, or, small things to compare
        with great, a little too Miltonic;
Its grandiloquence not sufficiently softened down by that
        copious admixture of commonplace
Which renders Bab Macaulay, James Montgomery and
        Mrs. Hemans so delightful;
Whilst on the other hand it exhibits, but too often alas! the
        directly opposite and worse fault
Of nude and barren simplicity, absence not of adornment
        alone but even of decent dress.
I'll not worry you with a host of examples; to a man of your
        sense one's as good as a thousand;
"Ex uno disce omnes," as Eneas said, wishing to save Dido
        time and trouble;
The very last line of your poem, the summing up of your whole work,

[*From the one, learn all*]

Where, if anywhere, there should be dignity and emphasis,
        something to make an impression
And ring in the ear of the reader after he has laid down the book
And be quoted by him to his children and children's children
        on his deathbed,
As an honored ancestor of mine, one of my predecessors in
        this very reviewer's chair,
Is said to have died with—no, not with the concluding verse
        of Homer's Iliad on his lips,
For Homer has by some fatality concluded his great poem
        much after your meagre fashion—
But with the magnificent couplet on his lips, which the judicious
        translator substitutes for the lame Homeric ending:
    "Such honors Iliam to her hero paid,
    And peaceful slept the mighty Hector's shade."
The very last line of your work, I say, the peroration of your poem,
So far from presenting us, like this fine verse, with something
        full and round and swelling
For ear and memory to take hold of and keep twirling about,
        barrel-organ-wise,
That is to say when ear and memory have, as they often have,
        nothing better to do,
Hasn't even sufficient pith in it for an indifferent prose period,
Exhibits such a deficiency of thew and sinew, not to say of soul
        and ethereal spirit,
Such a woful dearth of rough stuff and raw material, not to
        say of finish and top dressing,
That the reader cares but little either to catch a hold or keep
        a hold of it,
And it drops from between the antennae of his disappointed expectation
Pretty much in the same way as a knotless thread from
        between a housewife's fingers.

And yet when I consider how well adapted your "Home to his
          mother's house, private, returned" is
To take off the edge of the reading appetite, and with what
          right good will
After reading this verse one lays down the book without wishing
          it were longer,
I can't help correcting my first judgment and saying, with a
          smile, to myself:
"Well, after all, that finale's less injudicious than appears at first sight."
And now I have only to beg your kind excuse for the freedom
          of the observations
Which in my double capacity of friend of literature and
          literary men,
And clerk of the literary market, bound to protect the public
Against unsound, unwholesome or fraudulently made-up
          intellectual food,
I have felt it my duty to make on your, to me at least, very
          new and original work,
A work which, crude and imperfect as it is and full of marks
          of a beginner's hand,
Affords to the practised critic's eye indubitable evidences
          of a latent power
Sure to break forth as soon as the favorable opportunity
          presents itself
And astonish the world perhaps with a second—I was going
          to say Don Juan,
But, as I hate hyperbole and love to be within the mark,
I'll say—with a second Thabala or Antient Mariner or Excursion;
Glorious consummation! which the kind Fates have,
          no doubt, in reserve for you
If in the meantime you're content to live upon hope, and
          don't too much economize midnight oil.

SHE never in her whole life wrote one stanza,
She knew no Greek, no Latin, scarcely French,
She played not, danced not, sang not, yet when Death
His arms about her threw, to tear her from me,
I would have ransomed her, not Orpheus-like
With mine own song alone, but with *all* song,
Music and dance, philosophy and learning
Were ever, or to be were, in the world.

CLEVER people are disagreeable, always taking the advantage of you;
Stupid people are disagreeable, you never can knock anything
                                    into their heads;
Idle people are disagreeable, you must be continually amusing them;
Busy people are disagreeable, never at leisure to attend to you;
Extravagant people are disagreeable, always wanting to borrow of you;
Saving people are disagreeable, won't lay out a penny on you;
Obliging people are disagreeable, always putting you
                                    under a compliment;
Rude people are disagreeable, never stop rubbing you against the grain;
Religious people are disagreeable, always boring you with points
                                    of faith;
Irreligious people are disagreeable, no better than Turks and heathens;
Learned people are disagreeable, don't go by the rules of common sense;
Unlearned people are disagreeable, never can tell you what you
                                    don't already know;
Fashionable people are disagreeable, mere frivolity and emptiness;
Vulgar people are disagreeable, don't know how to behave themselves;
Wicked people are disagreeable, you're never safe in their company;
But no people are so disagreeable as your truly good and
                                    worthy people—
Slop-committee water-gruel, without a spice of wine or nutmeg,
Mawzy mutton overboiled, without pepper, salt, or mustard.

"IN the name of God we bind thee to this stake,
In the name of God heap fagots up about thee,
In the name of God set fire to them and burn thee
Alive and crying loud to heaven for succor,
And thus prove to the world the truthfulness
Of our own creed and how it mollifies
And fills with charity the human heart,
And that thy creed's as blasphemous as false,
Th' invention of the Devil, and by God
Permitted to his enemies and those
Who have no milk of kindness in their breasts."

Such words heard Huss and Latimer and Ridley,
Jerome of Prague and Cranmer and Socinus,
And such words, reader, thou shouldst hear tomorrow,
Hadst thou but courage to stand up against
The dominant creed, and were that creed less safe,
A trifle less safe, less securely seized
Of its honors, powers, immunities, and wealth.

O INSCRUTABLE justice and mercy and wisdom!
Unabashed in thy face looks the apple, the sinner;
The innocent pear droops its head, bears the shame.

HE died, and the emancipated soul
Flew upward, upward, till it came to—hell's gate;
Where it was told, that, having left at night,
It should have gone down, not have mounted upward,
For heaven, above all day, by night was downward.
But the soul being etherial could not sink down
Through the thick dense air, and but higher rose
The more it struggled to fly headlong downward.
So in compassion hell's gate-porter stowed it
In neighbouring Limbo with unchristened children's
Innocent helpless spirits, suicides,
And souls which, like itself, had gone astray,
There in asylum safe the tedious time
To while as best it might till mother church
Decided how at last to be disposed of
Convenient Limbo's church-perplexing spirits.

ONCE on a time a thousand different men
Together knelt before as many Gods
Each from the other different as themselves
Were different each from each, yet didn't fall out,
Or cut each others' throats amidst their prayers—
"Stop there! that never happened, or, if it did,
'Twas by a miracle; or if it happened
Really and in the way of nature, tell me
How, where, and when, what kind of men they were,
What kind of Gods—didn't even the Gods fall out?"
Not even the Gods; I'll tell thee how it was;
But art thou trusty? canst thou keep the secret?
"Yes yes." Then in thine ear: the thousand Gods
Had all the selfsame name; so every God,
Hearing no name invoked except his own,
Believed that every man of all the thousand
Worshipped him only; while each one of all
The thousand worshippers, hearing no name
Except his own God's name invoked, believed
That every one of all the whole nine hundred
Ninety and nine worshipped no God but his;
So all the thousand men together lived
In love and peace, as holding the same faith,
And of the thousand Gods not one was jealous.

from
Thalia Petasata,
or A foot-journey from Carlsruhe to Bassano
(1859)

LONG weeks the rain had lasted and but ceased
Early that morning, yet beneath our feet
Firm and scarce damp the well-made road of gneiss,
With white quartz grains and glassy hornblende sparkling,
And smooth as mansion avenue newly rolled.
Leaden the sky and lowering, the whole earth
Green and luxuriant with the fresh spring season
And long rains—ah, that the too liberal moisture
Wash not the pollen from the drooping halm,
And disappoint the sickle in July!
I fear, I fear; for even the North himself
Today blows damp and tepid, and the few
Hills that appear, refuse to acknowledge him
Or in his honor doff their misty caps.
    We leave the too straight highway and along
The hillside wind by Oberweier and Sulzbach,
Treading at every step on linden blossoms
And scarce-formed pears down beaten to the ground
By the preceding night's unpitying rain,
And, had the evening not been damp and misty,
Had seen from our advantage-ground away
Beyond the Hardtwald and Rhine panorama
To the Vosges plateaus and the setting sun:
As 'twas, we saw between us and the wood
The white steam-banner of the Basel train
Posting to Carlsruhe:—"Bear our friendly greeting
And long adieus"—we cried, and down the hill,
Warned by the pattering raindrops, our steps quickened,
And in the Golden Lamb in rural Malsch
Were safe in shelter within ten short minutes,
And looked out on the pelting rain and storm,
And supped on pancakes and twelve-kreuzer wine,
And, wearied by our journey of ten miles

Because unwonted, went to bed with daylight
And sound all night slept, and awoke next morning
To skies still dark and lowering, misty hills,
And dripping leaves and eaves and a wet day.

LET those, who will, enjoy the English bed
Of feather-stalks from which successive housemaids
Have pillaged to the last flock the fine down,
And English sheets in dirty water washed
And smelling of the suds; but, if thou lov'st me,
Give me th' Italian mattress broad and long,
Of fine, combed wool elastic; and the coarse
Hempen or linen sheets, washed in the fountain,
Lye-steeped, rinsed out, and in the hot sun dried,
And without mangle gloss or smoothing-iron's,
Crisp on the bed spread, white and fresh and sweet.
So said we or so thought, that night in Puschlaf,
As on our broad Italian mattresses
Substratified with springy maize, we stretched us,
Lengthwise to lie or crosswise, as we liked,
Or, if the humor took us so, diagonal.
But God disposes while short-sighted man
Proposes vain; a cow below our windows
Goes tinkle tinkle with her bell all night,
Driving away no doubt the noxious flies,
And not one wink we sleep, despite our sheets
Pure as the driven snow, despite our maize,
Our six-foot-wide wool mattresses despite.

I LIKE a long, straight, narrow, dusty road—
That is, in case it's neither very long,
Nor very dusty, and in case it's thickly
Planted on each side with tall, stately poplars
Pyramidal, luxuriant, green and whispering,
And not less than a hundred years old, each,
And casting down, each, its delicious shade
On the white, glaring dust, and, with its fellows,
Forming a vista through which at one end
Appears a steeple—not cocked on a church,
Like peacock's feather on the hat of a fool,
But on the firm ground built, and overtopping
The church beside it by some half dozen stories—
And at the other end the city's entrance
With busy people passing in and out,
And overhead, between the poplar tops,
A narrow stripe of blue, Italian sky,
From town to steeple stretched like a blue ribbon.

———————————

FARTHER on,
A stone erected by the way-side bids us
Pray for the soul of Gaetano Copri
Here cruelly, upon Good Friday night
Of the year eighteen hundred one and fifty,
By heartless villains waylaid, robbed and murdered;
His birth-place Vezza, thirty nine his years.
A death's-head and cross-bones attest the fact,
And warn the passer-by he too is mortal.
A little farther on, another stone,
With its death's-head and cross-bones, begs our prayers
For Giacomina Balzi on this spot

Dropped down dead suddenly May twenty-seventh,
In the year eighteen hundred of our Lord,
And of her age the sixtieth and ninth.
A third and fourth and fifth like marble stone,
With like death's-head and cross-bones, but without
Further inscription than the short initials
M. B., G. S., and B. T., and the dates,
Inform us Death has been upon this road
As busy as he's wont to be elsewhere,
And *sub silentio* beg a paternoster—
—In vain from us, too philosophical
To take in hand to change the unchangeable,
Or too religious to adore a God
Whose memory needs a flapper, or whose goodness
Lies hybernating cold till galvanized
By flattery's electric current sent
To heaven through prayer's trans-atmospheric cable.

———————————

ALL the next day we spend at the Pieve,
Visiting Baron Moll and dining with him;
A formal visit and a formal dinner,
With little of the heart on either side;
Neither his fault nor ours; for he's a baron,
And barons are by necessary nature
To us, as we to them, antipodistic;
For, what's a baron but a man, your brother,
By the hand taken and set up above you
To be above you and look down upon you,
If gentle tempered, condescendingly;
Insultingly, if, as far oftenest, rude?

[*in silence*]
So if thou'rt wise, plebeian! let consort
Baron with baron—proud eye to proud eye,
And to proud hand, proud hand—and open only
To thy plebeian brother thy whole heart;
And flatter not thyself thine infinitely
Superior learning, wisdom, moral worth
Will serve to countervail one single carat's
Deficiency of adventitious rank;
Nor should it; for it's not the whole man's weighed
Against the whole man, nor dost thou for comrade
Seek him who on the whole has most good points;
But the wise seek the wise, the learned the learned,
The rich the rich, and if the man of rank
The man of rank seeks, why should that offend?
Who is it shall throw at him the first stone?
And if he seek thee too because thou'rt moral
Or learned or wise, remember thou seek'st him
Because he's noble, and as he to thee
Always remains unwise, unlearned, immoral,
And in so far despised, so thou to him
Always remain'st ignoble and, as such,
Always despised; nice, delicate adjustment!
Respect on both sides and, on both, contempt.
On such *entente cordiale* well understood
The meanest subject dines even with his king,
And we with Baron Moll dine at Bezecca,
A mile from the Pieve, higher up
The Val di Ledro, where the Baron spends,
Villeggiaturing, the midsummer months,
Too hot for him at Villa on the Adige.
Villeggiatura I commend of all things,
Less for the purer air, than for the use,

Else never to aristocrat allowed,
Of his own limbs. Gods, but it's wondrous wondrous!
My Lord John or my Lord John's second cousin,
M. P. for the West-Riding, with his lustrous
Paris silk-hat, and gloves of kid unspotted
Adhering tighter than the natural skin
To his soap-scented, white and taper fingers—
So delicate, genteel, and feeble-limbed
He ventures not without supporting hand
Of lackey to ascend his well stuffed chariot,
Thence to look down on me, who use my feet,
Much wondering that I can, more that I choose;
But take the selfsame man villeggiaturing,
When the House breaks up and the Twelfth of August
Clears Pallmall and the Carlton, and pours down
God's wrath in fire and brimstone on the moors—
Behold him then with jacket velveteen,
And double-barrelled manton, pouch and shot-bag,
And gutta-percha boots, and squirrel cap,
Striding like Hercules, despising bog,
Despising heat and cold and wind and rain,
Courting fatigue and hard fare, glorying in
His aim unerring and sagacious pointer,
And counting up, with such as flush as Caesar
Counted his conquered Gallic provinces,
His five and twenty brace of slaughtered grouse,
And—strangest pride of all pride's Proteus forms!—
Himself congratulating that he's turned
—Mind, for the season only; for, the whole
Long year beside, he's Christian civilisation's
Champion and paragon—into a savage.
Today however's not the Twelfth of August,
And if it were there are few grouse or none

Here in the Val di Ledro, so the Baron's
Trophies today when he comes home to dinner,
Begrimed like Hector's ghost that to Eneas
Comes at midnight to tell him Troy is taken,
Are, not a bag of twenty brace of grouse,
But a poor, paltry string of some half dozen
Grizzled hare scuts—spoils not enough to win,
And scarce enough to save, a Nimrod's fame,
But evidence, as Holy Writ conclusive,
Of the animus to kill, not for the sake
Of necessary food, or to destroy
Pernicious vermin, but with one's own hands
To kill for pastime and sweet recreation.

I LIKE society, I like a friend,
But I don't like society unequal;
I cannot cringe and say:— "Ay, ay, my Lord;
That's true, my Lord; your Lordship's always right."
And who says so to me, to me's the fox
Who knows that to my cheese the shortest way
Lies through my vanity, to me's the poodle
Erect upon his hind legs dancing round,
With slavering jaws, and eyes turned toward the bone.
I like society, I like a friend,
He need not be a Damon or Orestes,
For I no Pythias am, nor Pylades;
No Socrates need he be, for I, alas!
Am neither the wise Jew nor wise Athenian;
But he must be one who, upon a pinch,
A crown, or, in a case extreme, two crowns
Would lend me without interest; a man

Who, if a tree were falling upon both,
Would, while he ran himself, bid me run too;
A man who, if the talk be of the Devil,
At least can tell you whether it's his right foot,
Or left's the cloven one; a man, in short,
Neither much better furnished, heart or head,
Nor much worse furnished than I am myself.
To such a man, as soon as met, I swear
Eternal friendship; and with such a man,
If, as most probable, through some of Nature's
Cross-purposes, I never meet, why then
One good at least is clear—we'll never quarrel.

from
Menippea
(1866)

I SAW him pick it up; it was a rag
Worth nothing, yet he picked it up and stowed it
Away into his pouch, as thou wouldst gold.
Misery was in his face, and in the act,
And in the shame with which he strove, in vain,
The act to hide. My very heart bled for him,
And with mine eye I followed him until
In, at a door more wretched than himself,
Tottering and slow and sad, he disappeared.
Twice, in my dreams, since then I've seen his frail,
Stooped, trembling figure; more than twice since then
Have, to my waking self, hoped he was dead
And out of suffering, and no longer, more
Than ever impious atheist by his reasoning,
Against God's goodness and God's providence,
By the mere fact of his being alive, blasphemed.

Julian and Gallus,
In the Castle of Macellum

Julian
LIKE, as an egg's, life's two ends to each other:
Blind, helpless, speechless, at one end we enter,
Not knowing where we are, or whence we come;
Blind, helpless, speechless, exit at the other—
Who has come back to tell us why or whither?

Gallus
Lazarus, for one.

Julian
And what did Lazarus say?

Gallus
Nothing; seemed not to know he had been away.

The Lord and Adam,
In the Garden of Eden

The Lord
—FOR, dust thou art, and shalt to dust return.

Adam
If dust I am, and shall to dust return,
All's right. I shall return to what I am.

The Lord
Thou'rt quite too literal; I love a trope.

Adam
That's more than I do. I must fairly own
I don't like to have sand thrown in mine eyes.
Why make that harder still to understand,
Which, in itself, is hard? The plainest speech
Pleases me most.

The Lord
                    He'll not make a bad Quaker. *[aside]*
—And for thy sake the serpent too is cursed,
Shall on his belly go, and eat the dust.

Adam
That's a trope too, no doubt.

The Lord

Why, half and half;
Trope, he shall eat the dust; but literal
And matter of fact, he shall go on his belly.

Adam

Excuse me—on his back; for on his belly
He goes at present and has always gone.

The Lord

Belly or back, 's small difference in a serpent;
From either he'll know how to bruise thy heel.

Adam

But I'll go in a carriage, ride on horseback,
Or, if I go on foot, wear leather boots.

The Lord

Literal again! It would have saved some trouble,
To have put a few grains more of poetry
Into the dull prose of thy composition.

Adam

It can't be helped now; but next time you're making
A thing, like me, with an immortal soul
—For I'm none of your dust, I'm bold to tell you,
But an ethereal spirit in a case—
'Twere well you'd make him with sufficient wit
To understand your flights of poetry,
Or, if not, that you'd talk to him in prose.

Old-World Stories

I.

The Creation

ON the day before the first day,
God was tired with doing nothing,
And determined to rise early
On the next day and do something.

So, upon the next day, God rose
Very early, and the light made—
You must know that until that day
God had always lived in darkness:—

"Bravo! bravo! that's a good job,"
Said God, when his eye the light caught;
"Now, I think, I'll try and make me
A convenient place to live in."

So, upon the next day, God rose
At the dawn of light, and heaven made,
And, from that day forward, never
Wanted a snug box to live in:—

"Well! a little work is pleasant,"
Said God, "and besides it's useful;
What a pity I've so long sat
Dumping, mumping, doing nothing!"

So, upon the third day, God made
This round ball of land and water,
And, with right thumb and forefinger,
Set it, like teetotum, spinning;

Spinning, twirling like teetotum,
Round and round about, the ball went,
While God clapped his hands, delighted,
And called th' angels to look at it.

Who made th' angels? if you ask me,
I reply:—that's more than I know;
For if God had, I don't doubt but
He'd have put them in his catalogue;

But no matter—some one made them,
And they came about him flocking,
Wondering at the sudden fit of
Manufacturing that had taken him:—

"It's a pretty ball," they all said;
"Do, pray, tell us what's the use of it;
Won't you make a great many of them?
We would like to see them trundling."

"Wait until tomorrow," said God,
"And I think I'll show you something;
This is quite enough for one day,
And you know I'm but beginning."

So, about noon, on the fourth day,
God called th' angels all about him,
And showed them the great big ball he'd
Made to give light to the little one.

"What!" said th' angels, "such a big ball,
Just to give light to a little one!
That's bad management, and you know, too,
You had plenty of light without it."

"Not quite plenty," said God, snappish,
"For the light I made the first day,
Although good, was rather scanty,
Scarce enough for me to work by.

"And besides how was it possible,
If I had not made the big ball,
To have given the little one seasons,
Days and years and nights and mornings?

"So, you see, there was nothing for it
But to fix the little ball steady,
And, about it, set the big one
Topsy-turvying as you here see."

"It's the big ball we see steady,
And the little one round it whirling,"
Said the angels, by the great light
Dazzled, and their eyebrows shading:—

"None of your impertinence," said God,
Growing more vexed every moment;
"I know that, as well as you do,
But I don't choose you should say it.

"I have set the big ball steady,
And the little one spinning round it,
But I've told you just the opposite,
And the opposite you must swear to."

"Anything you say, we'll swear to,"
Said the angels, humbly bowing;
"Have you anything more to show us?
We're so fond of exhibitions."

"Yes," said God, "what was deficient
In the lighting of the little ball,
With this pretty moon I've made up,
And these little, twinkling stars here."

"Wasn't the big ball big enough?" said
With simplicity the angels:—
"Couldn't, without a miracle," said God,
"Shine at once on back and front side."

"There you're quite right," said the angels,
"And we think you show your wisdom,
In not squandering miracles on those
Who believe your word without them.

"But do tell us why you've so far
From your little ball put your little stars;
One would think they didn't belong to it;
Scarce one in a thousand shines on it."

"To be sure I could have placed them
So much nearer," said God smiling,
"That the little ball would have been as
Well lit with some millions fewer;

"But I'd like to know of what use
To th' Omnipotent such economy—
Can't I make a million million stars
Quite as easily as one star?"

"Right, again," said th' angels; "there can
Be no manner of doubt about it."
"That's all now," said God; "tomorrow,
Come again, and ye shall more see."

When the angels came the next day,
God indeed had not been idle,
And they saw the little ball swarming
With all kinds of living creatures.

There they went in pairs, the creatures,
Of all sizes, shapes and colors,
Stalking, hopping, leaping, climbing,
Crawling, burrowing, swimming, flying,

Squealing, singing, roaring, grunting,
Barking, braying, mewing, howling,
Chuckling, gabbling, crowing, quacking,
Cawing, croaking, buzzing, hissing.

Such assembly there has never,
From that day down, been on earth seen;
From that day down, such a concert
There has never been on earth heard;

For, there, ramping, and their maker
Praising in their various fashions,
Were all God's created species,
All except the fossilized ones;

For whose absence on that great day,
The most likely cause assigned yet,
Is that they were quite forgotten
And would not go uninvited.

But let that be as it may be,
All th' unfossilized ones were there,
Striving which of them would noisiest
Praise bestow upon their maker.

"Well," said th' angels, when they'd looked on
Silently, some time, and listened;
"Well, you surely have a strange taste;
What did you make all these queer things for?"

"Come tomorrow and I'll show you,"
Said God, gleeful, his hands rubbing;
"All you've yet seen's a mere nothing
To what you shall see tomorrow."

So, when th' angels came the next day
All tiptoe with expectation,
And stretched necks and eyes and ears out
Towards the new world, God said to them:—

"There he is, my last and best work;
There he is, the noble creature;
I told you, you should see something;
What do you say now? have I word kept?"

"Where, where is he?" said the angels;
"We see nothing but the little ball
With its big ball, moon and little stars
And queer, yelping, capering kickshaws."

"I don't well know what you mean by
Kickshaws," said God, scarcely quite pleased,
"But, among my creatures yonder,
Don't you see one nobler figure?

"By his strong, round, tail-less buttocks,
And his flat claws you may know him,
Even were he not so like me
That we might pass for twin brothers."

"Now we see him," said the angels;
"How is 't possible we o'erlooked him?
He's indeed your very image,
Only smaller and less handsome."

"So I hope the mystery's cleared up,"
Said God, with much self-complacence,
"And you are no longer puzzled
What I've been about, these six days."

"Even th' Almighty," said the angels,
"May be proud of such chef-d'oeuvre,
Such magnificent and crowning
Issue of a six days' labor.

"But we're curious to know whether
He's as good inside as outside,
As substantial and enduring
As he's fair to see, and specious."

Here a deep sigh rent God's bosom,
And a shade came o'er God's features:—
"Ah," he cried, "were ye but honest,
And no traitor stood amongst ye!

"Then indeed this were a great work,
Then indeed I were too happy;
Ah! it's too bad, downright too bad,
But I'll—shall I? yes, I'll let you;

"Let you disappoint and fret me,
Let you disconcert my whole plan—
Why, of all my virtues, should I
Leave unpractised only patience?

"There he is, my noblest, best work;
Take him, do your pleasure with him;
After all, perhaps I'll find some
Means to patch my broken saucer.

"Now begone! don't let me see you
Here again, till I send for you;
I'm tired working, and intend to
Rest my weary bones tomorrow."

So God lay late on the next day,
And, the whole day long, did nothing
But reflect upon his ill luck
And the great spite of the angels;

And God said:—"Because I've rested
All this seventh day, and done nothing,
Each seventh day shall be kept holy
And a day of rest, for ever."

And as God said and commanded,
So it is now, and still shall be:
All hard work done on each seventh day,
To each first day all respect shown.

Old-World Stories

II.

Adam and Eve

NOW I'll tell you—story second—
How God made his noblest, best work—
Made the man and made the woman,
With the strong, round, tail-less buttocks.

God took dust—about three bushels
Very fine dust, without mixture
Of quartz rubbish, grit or pebble—
Wet, and kneaded it, with water.

—Nay, nay; I don't mean such water
As Jove, Mercury and Neptune
Wet the cow's hide with, when all three
Set about to make Orion—

With rain water God the dust mixed,
Kneaded, moulded into figure,
Till head, face and trunk and four limbs
Wore his own most perfect likeness.

Then in through its nose God blew till
All its lungs were full of God's breath,
And its heart went pit-pat, pit-pat,
And it stood up, on its two legs,

And, about it, looked, and wondered,
And a hop step and three jumps took,
Chattered like a daw or magpie,
Like a kitten, playful capered.

Now there was in Eden, eastward,
Planted by God's self, a garden;
There, it was, God put his image,
Bade him live in it, dress and keep it:

Not because he was a gardener,
Or knew anything of gardening,
Nor because the garden needed
To be dressed or taken care of;

For the ground had not been cursed yet,
And produced no thorns nor thistles;
Every thing went of itself right;
All was good and in perfection;

But he put him there to tempt, and
Try if he could catch him napping,
Laid a regular trap for him—
Sure enough, he fell plump into it.

Now you'll say that God was cunning,
When I tell you how he did it:
—Like as to himself he made Man,
He didn't make Man half so cunning—

In the middle of the garden,
Full in the man's sight he set a
Tree with goodly apples laden,
Fair to see, and fragrant smelling,

Then said to the man:—"Thou shalt not,
Fair although they be, and fragrant,
Eat or touch one single apple—
Upon pain of death, thou shalt not.

"Eat thou mayst of all the other
Apples in the garden growing,
But of this tree if thou touchest
Even one apple, thou'rt a dead man."

So God said, and brought a deep, sound
Sleep on Adam, his beloved son;
Then, while he was sleeping, came and
Opened one, no matter which, side;

Cautious opened, and took out a
Rib too many he had given him;
Then the wound, as cautious, healed up,
Adam never once perceiving.

In the rib God flesh and bone had,
Ready to his hand provided,
So it took but little trouble
To make out of it a new man.

Twin to twin was never liker,
Than the new man God made of it,
And to Adam gave, to be his
Loving helpmate, Eve, first woman.

So far, so good; if the man's stiff,
Of himself won't touch the apple,
Woman's curious, and will likely
Nibble, and persuade her husband.

Pretty sure, now; but to make still
Surer, safer, God a serpent
Put into the garden with them,
Full of subtilty and malice,

And, because the serpent could not,
Without knowledge of their language,
Use his forked tongue to beguile them,
How to speak their language, taught him.

What their language was, I know not;
Hebrew, Sanscrit or Chaldean—
Some say it was Paradisiac;
Celtic, some; some, Abyssinian—

But the serpent knew, and thus said
To the woman in her language:—
"It's a very pretty story
God has told you and your husband,

"That ye shall die in the day ye
Taste, or touch, one of these apples.
Pshaw! don't mind him; he'd fain keep all
Wisdom to himself, and knowledge.

"What for are they, but for eating?
Who's to eat, but you and Adam?
Put your hand forth, pluck and eat one,
And be wise as he, and knowing."

What should Eve do, silly woman,
Who knew neither good nor evil,
Could not tell what either meant till
She had first the apple tasted?

And the serpent was so pretty,
And so sweetly spoke her language,
And was one of God's own creatures,
In God's garden, sporting, with her;

And the apple, on the branch, there,
Hung so ripe and round and mellow,
And the tree was by God's own hand
Planted, and made grow so near her;

And she had never even so much as
Dreamt that God, a jealous God was—
A designing, jealous God was,
Who would lay a trap to catch her;

Who would rain down fire and brimstone
On her great-great-great-grandchildren;
Who would slay, in one night, all the
First-born in the land of Egypt;

Who would cut off every soul in
Canaan and the plains of Jordan;
Who would not spare even his own heir,
Or the bitter cup pass from him.

So she stretched—she stretched her hand out,
Plucked and eat, and gave to Adam,
Who, as God from the beginning
Well had guessed, eat at her bidding.

Then, at last, their eyes were opened,
—All too late and to no purpose—
And they knew what they had done was
Evil, and would be their ruin.

And they said, one to the other,
Knowing now both good and evil:—
"Well! it surely was a foul trick;
Who'd have thought God would have done it.

"He is not the God we thought him,
But a cruel, wicked, bad God;
Come, make haste and in the thicket
Let us hide us from his anger."

Ah! they little knew the God from
Whom they thought to hide their faces;
He was in the garden spying,
—Taking, as he said, a cool walk—

Saw them pluck and eat the apple,
Saw the whole thing, how it happened,
Then, as if he had seen nothing,
Looking simple, called them to him,

And, what they had been doing, asked them.
When he heard, Lord! if you'd seen him,
How he cursed and swore and threatened,
How he vowed he'd have their two lives,

Damned the woman, and the man damned,
Damned the serpent worse than either,
Cursed the very ground they stood on,
The poor ground that had done nothing;

Thorns, it should bring forth, and thistles;
In his sweat, the man should till it;
Pain and sorrow should attend the
Hapless woman in child-bearing.

Then God drove both man and woman
Out before him, and a guard of
Cherubim in Eden, eastward,
With a flaming, fiery sword placed.

High and low, on every side round,
Day and night, the fiery sword flamed—
Shut them out, for ever shut them
Out of Eden's happy garden.

And the two went forth to wander
And spread, far and wide, the story,
And behind them in the garden
Left the serpent cozy nestled.

Old-World Stories

III.

Cain and Abel

STORY third is but a short one:
Cain was Abel's elder brother;
Children they were both of Adam,
Eve, of both the boys, was mother.

Bad boys both were; God had taken
Good care they should not be good ones,
For he had cursed both their parents,
Cursed the very ground they stood on.

These two bad boys brought God offerings,
—Fondest, still, to bring God offerings,
Are the worst boys, and most pains take
Always to keep God on their side—

Of the ground's fruit Cain brought offerings;
Firstlings of the flock, brought Abel;
God a lover was of lamb's flesh,
Didn't care much for ears of green corn.

So God showed respect to Abel,
Said he liked his roast lamb vastly,
And his back turned on the green ears,
Bid Cain give them to the cattle.

Cain grew wroth—was it a wonder?—
Wroth with God and wroth with Abel,
And the countenance of Cain fell,
And he slew his brother Abel.

And God asked Cain where was Abel,
Just as if God did not know well,
And Cain answered:—"Go and seek him;
Am I then my brother's keeper?"

Then God said:—"I've heard the voice of
Abel's blood up from the ground cry.
Thou hast slain him. I expected
Better from thy parents' son, Cain.

"What use now in all the pains I
Took to teach them to distinguish
Good from evil, that they might know
How to rear up virtuous children?

"Some excuse there was for them, if
In their ignorance, they offended;
But there's none at all for thee, Cain;
With eyes open thou hast done this.

"So thou'rt damned: begone for ever!
Out before my face I hunt thee;
And upon thee set my mark, that
Every man may know and shun thee.

"Sevenfold vengeance I will take on
Him that lays on Cain a finger.
Out! begone!" and God drove Cain forth,
Outlawed, with the mark upon him.

Now there was not, in the whole world,
Other man than Cain and Adam;
Other woman, in the whole world,
There was not than Eve, his mother;

So the mark didn't do Cain much harm,
And he went into the land of
Nod, and married, or, as some say,
Into Nod's land took his wife with him.

Who his wife was, I don't well know,
But suspect she was an angel—
Of an angel Cain had need, if
Ever man had need of angel;

But in Nod's land Cain a son had,
And in Nod's land built a city,
Enoch—so called from his son's name—
'Tmust have been but a small city,

For, to build it, Cain had but his
Own two bare hands and his wife's two
And his little son's—with the mark on him,
Who, do you think, besides, would help him,

Even if Nod's land had been peopled,
Which it was not? so Cain's city
Was as big as Cain could build it
With his wife's help and his little son's;

Not so big, be sure, as Rome was
Built upon the banks of Tiber
By another and a worse Cain,
Whom God never dreamt of outlawing,

But to heaven took, and rewarded
With a crown of life and glory,
And his city made to flourish,
And reign mistress of the wide world.

Like a knotless thread, my story
Here drops from between my fingers,
For what more Cain in the land of
Nod did, or elsewhere, 's not written.

Old-World Stories

Abraham

Part Third

"LEAD us not into temptation,"
Is a prayer we offer up to
God Almighty, night and morning,
And, no doubt, there is some use in it;

For, if God one single fault has,
It's that he's so fond of tempting,
And from the right path seducing,
His but too confiding children.

Ah, how happy we might be now,
What a different world have of it,
Had but Eve the Lord's Prayer practised,
She and Adam, night and morning!

But they did not; they had too much
Faith in God's own innate goodness,
To believe there could be use in
Begging God not to mislead them.

What the consequence, I need not
Tell those who so sorely feel it;
How successful the Creator's
Pitfall for his own creation.

Abraham too—but I suspect that
Abraham knew God was but joking,
And the joke met with a like joke,
Didn't at all mean to kill Isaac.

Hear the story; for yourselves judge;
Don't take my opinion of it;
These are times when 'gentle, semple'
—Young and old—are all alike wise:

In one of those entertaining
Conversaziones God used
Now and then to hold with Abraham,
He's reported to have thus said:—

"Abraham, I've a woman's longing
For the smell of a roast child's flesh;
Thou'st a son—a loved son—Isaac;
Kill and roast, and let me smell him.

"Since I first smelt Abel's roast lamb,
I have loved the smell of roast meat;
But I hear, of all roast meats there's
None so savory smells as roast child."

"Lord," said Abraham, "be not angry,
But if thou to child's flesh takest,
How am I henceforth to know thee
Different from Baal and Chemosh?"

"Answer me this, first," replied God;
"Why mayn't I be Abraham's God still,
Though I choose to treat my nostrils,
This once, to a sniff of roast child?

"It's not in itself a thing's right,
But it's right because God does it,
Or, which comes much to the same thing,
Right because God bids it be done.

"To be sure, to kill and roast a
Child, is murder, in your law's eye,
And to kill and roast one's own child,
Worse than murder, twenty times worse;

"But the case is changed when God bids,
And—to quote a tongue, beforehand,
I'll, one day, deal much in—Deus
Est justificationi.

"Then to kill and roast your own child,
Proves not only your obedience,
But your righteousness and faith and
Firm conviction of God's goodness,

"And that God shall not in vain ask
You, his servant, to do for him
That which those who worship Baal and
Chemosh, cheerfully for them do.

[*?: God exists as justification*]

"Up! make haste! and on the mountain
I shall show thee in Moriah,
Kill and roast thy loved son, Isaac;
High the mountain, and the smell will

"Reach to heaven, and glad my nostrils,
And I will remember Abraham,
And according to my promise,
Bless, and make a great man of him."

Further answer Abraham made none
—Abraham was, you know, a wise man—
But his ass got, and his son took,
And the wood, and two men, with him.

And set out and, on the third day,
To the foot, came, of the mountain
God had told him of, and left there
Both the donkey and the two men,

And said to them:—"Here abide ye,
While my son and I go higher
Up the mountain, God to worship;
Worship over, we will come back,

"With the blessing of the God who
Hates a lie as he loves Abraham,
And has sworn to bless the whole earth
In my son, my loved son, Isaac."

This said, Abraham took the wood and
Bound it on the back of Isaac,
And went up the mountain with him,
Knife in one hand, fire in the other.

"There's one thing we have forgot," said
Isaac simply, as they went up;
"Here's the knife, the wood, the kindling;
But the lamb, papa, where is it?"

"God is good, my son," said Abraham,
"And will with a lamb provide us."
"Is it good in God," said Isaac,
"To provide a lamb for killing?

"Doesn't it hurt the pretty lamb to
Cut its throat with a great, sharp knife?
God is not good, or he would not
Even so much as let you kill it."

"Every thing is good that God does,
Or bids do," said Abraham, drily;
"Here's the place;" and, with the word, the
Wood untied from Isaac's shoulder,

And, with Isaac's help, an altar
Built of sods and stones, and on it
Laid the wood, and on the wood laid,
Hand and foot bound—his son Isaac.

You have heard how Agamemnon
Could not bear to look upon the
Spouting heart's blood of his daughter,
But his face wrapped in his mantle,

While into Iphigenia's
Bared breast Calchas plunged the dagger—
Ah, faint-hearted Agamemnon!
Weak as his own potsherd idols.

Abraham, servant of the true God,
Has a different heart, and in his
Own hand takes the knife and lifts high,
And is in the act of striking,

When—blessed, lucky chance for Isaac—
God remembers, on a sudden,
That it's in the seed of Isaac,
He has sworn to bless the whole earth,

And calls down from heaven:—"Stop, Abraham;
Thou hast done enough to please me;
With the animus God's contented,
Doesn't require the actual murder.

"That thou'rt faithful, thou hast well proved,
And in future to be trusted
To do this, or more than this, if
Need require it, in my service.

"Therefore I will multiply thee,
Greatly bless and multiply thee,
As the sand upon the sea shore,
As the stars of heaven, in number."

Abraham stopped and looked about, and
Saw a ram caught in the thicket
By its horns, and went and took it
—There was no policeman near him—

And upon the altar killed and
Roasted it, in place of Isaac,
And God put up with the smell of
Roasted ram, instead of roast child's.

So the sacrifice went on well;
God was pleased and so was Abraham;
And, when all was over, Isaac
Wiped his eyes, and whimpered "Amen!"

And that same hour God determined,
—Should he ever be so happy
As to have a son born to him,
And that son, by good luck, turn out

To be of so gentle nature
As in all things to submit him,
Unresisting, uncomplaining,
To his father's will and pleasure—

Not, indeed, to take the knife in-
To his own hand, Abraham fashion,
—Foolish people might an outcry
Raise against so high-flown virtue—

But into the hands deliver
Of his ministers, to kill and
Offer up, as a sin offering,
On the altar of his father:—

"So shall all the world acknowledge,"
Said God to himself, complacent,
"Better father there was never
Than myself, excepting Abraham;

"Nor, to horrid Moloch, ever
Offered in the vale of Tophet,
Purer or more spotless victim
Than I've offered to myself up;

"With whose guiltless blood I'll smear the
Sharp edge of my sword of justice,
With whose guiltless blood I'll quench the
Seething of my furious anger;

"With whose guiltless blood I'll wash the
Stains out of his guilty brethren;
With whose guiltless blood I'll sprinkle
The repentent, contrite sinner."

Thus God to himself, while Abraham
Went, with Isaac, down the mountain,
And the ass found, and the two men,
Waiting for him where he had left them.

"So the master has brought the lad back,
After worship, as he promised;"
Whispered, as they went along, one
Of the two men to his comrade.

"To be sure!" replied his comrade,
Whispering back; "Why mayn't the master
Tell truth sometimes—by mistake, or
When a lie won't serve his purpose?"

"True or false," still in a whisper,
Said the first of the two speakers,
"Sure as Father Abraham's in it,
There's a trick in it, top or bottom."

"Old Time's curious, and will find out,
If he can," replied the other,
"And is honest and will truly,
Good or bad, tell what he finds out."

So they whispered on the way home,
Abraham's two men, tittle tattle;
And you may be sure that Isaac,
When he got home, wasn't quite silent;

But no matter whether it was
Isaac blabbed or Time that found out,
You've the story as I heard it;
Not one word of it's my invention.

Life's Minutes

A MINUTE—and a minute—and a minute—
Until the last; and then—"What then?" Why, nothing;
Unless, indeed, last minute's not last minute,
And what's come to an end is not yet ended.

World's Minutes

A MINUTE—and a minute—and a minute—
Until the last; and then—"What then?" Why, nothing;
What except nothing can come after last
Minute, not come while anything exists?
For time is but a property of thing,
—Belongs to thing, like number or extension—
Or, if you please, a mode of viewing thing,
An aspect under which things are compared,
And dies away and vanishes, with thing.

WELL! I'll be patient, to myself I said,
And, though it's hard, do what I can to bear it,
Not doubting but it's all to end in good.
And yet, methinks, and with respect be it said,
Heaven did not take exactly the right way
To have me patient, giving me in hand
The ill, and only promising the good.
Ah, if instead of setting the cart so
Before the horse, it had into my hand
Given the good, and promised me the ill,
What perfect model I had been of patience!
With what sure hope looked forward to the future!

I

WHO'S the great sinner? He, who gave the power
And will to sin, and knew both would be used.

II

Who's the great sinner? He, to whose sole will
Sinner and sin alike owe their existence.

III

Who's the great sinner? He, who, being Omniscient,
Foresees all sins, and, being Omnipotent,
Can, if he please, prevent them and does not—
Nay, not alone does not, but punishes;
And—one tic farther still, one farther tic
Incredible—when punishment's no use.

Cradle Hymn,
Suggested by Dr. Watts's

"HUSH, my babe, lie still and slumber;
    Holy angels guard thy bed,
Heavenly blessings, without number,
    Gently falling on thy head,"

None so heavy as to break it—
    Hush, my babe, and nothing fear;
God thy little soul won't take yet,
    Still a while will leave thee here;

Here to struggle and to scramble
    Through the world as thou mayst best,
Torn by rose and torn by bramble—
    Hush, my babe, and take thy rest.

Don't, my babe, don't make wry faces,
    Keep them for the teething fit,
That first blessing Heaven's to send thee,
    If thou liv'st to eat a bit.

That's my good babe! now thou'rt quiet,
    I can hardly hear thy breath—
With my heart's blood I would buy it,
    Thou might'st so sleep on till death,

Nothing seeing, nothing hearing,
    Of the blessings Heaven lets fall—
Be they light or be they heavy,
    So thou best escap'st them all;

Nothing seeing, nothing hearing,
    Of the angels round thy bed,
Or how much it is, or little,
    Guardian angels stand in stead.

Ah! my child, might'st thou but sleep so
    Till thou drewest thy latest breath,
Thy sad mother need not weep so,
    Or so hate the thought of death,

Death, the grand finale blessing,
    Heaven upon all heads lets fall;
Let thy mother feel it double,
    So thou feel'st it not at all;

So thou'rt spared the pang of parting
    From thy nearest, dearest friend,
Whether thou'rt left here to mourn her,
    Or she's left to mourn thine end.

Might we but together sleep out
    Our brief night's existence frail,
Not be wakened up ere midnight,
    Each to hear the other's wail,

When the scythe-armed guardian angel
        Separates the locked embrace,
And one's left to mourn the other's
        Ever fresh remembered face!

Sleep on, babe, ere thou hast learned yet
        How like sleep is unto death;
Sleep on, babe, ere thou hast felt yet
        How life shortens with each breath;

Sleep on soundly ere the dreams come,
        Which disturb the soundest sleep;
Sleep on soundly ere the tears come,
        Thou must, if thou livest, weep.

Sleep, my babe, on; wake not up yet
        The forbidden fruit to eat;
Good and evil both are bitter,
        Life itself's a bitter sweet.

....."Nullis inclusit limina portis.
Nocte dieque patent....

....

Nulla quies intus, nullaque silentia parte."

Is it just in Heaven to favor so the eyes
With lids to keep out dust and glare and flies,
And leave the poor ears open, night and day,
To all each chattering fool may choose to say,
To all assaults of sturdy hurdygurd,
And grand-piano octave, chord, and third,
And rapid volley of well-quavered note,
Out of wide gaping, husband-seeking throat,
And fiddle squeak, and railway whistle shrill,
Big drum and little drum and beetling mill,
Trumpet and fife, triangle and trombone,
And hiss and shout and scream and grunt and groan?
Be gracious, Heaven! and, if no law forbid,
Grant the distracted ear such share of lid
That we may sometimes soundly sleep at night,
Not kept awake until the dawning light,
By rattling window-sash, or miauling cat,
Or howling dog, or nibbling mouse or rat,
Or cooped-up capon fain like cock to crow,
Or carts that down the paved street clattering go,
Or nurse, in the next room, and sickly child,
Warbling by turns their native woodnotes wild.

[Ovid, Metamorphoses xii. 45-48: *Fame has shut up the
thresholds to her house with no doors. Night and day they stand
open...There is no quiet within and silence is in no part.*]

Judge us not by thyself, who darest not sleep,
But open always, day and night, must keep
Both eye and ear, to see and hear how go
All things above the clouds, and all below;
Lids for thine ears, as for thine eyes, were worse
Than useless, an impediment and curse;
We, with less care, our eyes are free to close
At night, or for an after-dinner doze,
And for this purpose thou hast kindly given,
And with a bounty worthy of high Heaven,
Each eye a pair of lids. One lid might do
For each ear, if thou wilt not hear of two,
One large, well fitting lid; and night and day,
As bound in duty, we will ever pray;
And thou with satisfaction shalt behold
Our ears no less protected from the cold
Than our dear eyes, and never more need'st fear
That to thy word we turn a hard, deaf ear;
Never more fear that discord should arise
And jealous bickerings between ears and eyes,
Both members of one body corporate,
Both loyal subjects of one church and state;
Never more see us, on a frosty day,
Stuffing in cotton, or hear caviller say:
"I'd like to know why fallen less happy lot
On ear than on snuffbox and mustardpot;
What is it ever ear thought or ear did,
To disentitle it to its share of lid?"
Earlids, kind Heaven, or who knows what—? But no!
Silence, rebellious tongue, and let ear go
And plead its own case. Lidless, Heaven's own ear,
And, whether it will or not, must always hear.

Liberty, Equality, Fraternity

MY brothers are my equals; God's the same
Kind, good, considerate God to all his children,
Who've, every one, the same rights as myself.
Of course I don't include among God's children
Having the same rights as myself, my sisters;
I'd rather die, and go to heaven offhand,
Where neither hes nor shes find entrance ever,
But only its—the paradise of neuters—
Than by the sexus sequior so be swamped.
Nature abhors a vacuum; I, a bloomer.
Hurrah then for FRATERNITY! hurrah!
For LIBERTY hurrah, and EQUAL RIGHTS!
To hell with SORORIETY! down! down!
We're all alike God's children; God's the same
Kind, even-handed parent to us all,
Rich, poor, and young and old, unlearned and learned,
Wise, fool, and good and bad—except the women.

[the inferior sex]

BY what mistake were pigeons made so happy,
So plump and fat and sleek and well content,
So little with affairs of others meddling,
So little meddled with? say, collared dog,
And hard worked ox, and horse still harder worked,
And caged canary, why, uncribbed, unmaimed,
Unworked and of its will lord absolute,
The pigeon sole has free board and free quarters,
Till at its throat the knife, and pigeon pie
Must smoke ere noon upon the parson's table;
Say, if ye can; I cannot, for the life o' me;
But, wheresoe'er I go, I find it so;
The pigeon of all things that walk or fly
Or swim or creep, the best cared-for and happiest;
Ornament ever fresh and ever fair
Of castle and of cottage, palace roof
And village street, alike, and stubble field,
And every eye and volute of the minster;
Philosopher's and poet's and my own
Envy and admiration, theme and riddle;
Emblem and hieroglyphic of the third
Integral unit of the Trinity;
Not even by pagan set to heavier task
Than draw the car of Venus; since the deluge
Never once asked to carry in the bill,
And by the telegraph and penny-post
Released for ever from all charge of letters.

Striking a light, at night

"FIRST for the Bible, then the printing-press,
Most for the lucifer match, the Gods I bless;
Without the other two, at dead of night,
What were the first?" I said, and struck a light.

from
Poematia
(1866)

BLESSED be the man who first invented chairs!
And doubly blessed, the man who beds invented!
But blessed above them both and praised for ever,
By sick and well, young, old, and rich and poor,
By grave and gay, and ignorant and learned,
By lazy and by idle and by tired,
And most, by all who love, like me, to loll,
The livelong day through, trilling maudlin verses,
Th' ingenious man, if man indeed he were
And not divine, who first invented thee,
Half bed, half chair, delicious, spring-stuffed sofa!
Stretched at my ease on thee, I envy not
Turkish divan or carpet, kingly throne,
Or lectulus of Pliny or Lucullus
In Ostian villa or by Pausilippo;
Nay, envy scarce the hyacinthine couch
From which, half raised upon his elbow, Adam
Leaned over Eve, enamoured, kissed her cheek,
And bade her waken out of her first sleep
And greet a second day in paradise.
My Muse's visits I receive on thee,
Semi-recumbent, make her sit beside me,
And chat and banter with her to no end.
On thee I make my toilet, sit on thee
And eat and drink, and stretch me out to sleep.
Thou art my bed, my prie-dieu, chair and stool,
My bookcase and my cash-drawer and my wardrobe;
On thee I'll live, and when Death, at the last,
Comes looking for me, laid on thee he'll find me,
And thou shalt be my coffin and my bier,
And share with me the long night of the tomb.

I SAW, in Dresden, on a windy day,
A man and woman walking side by side,
—I tell a plain fact, not a poet's story,
And to my reader's judgment leave the moral—
He on his arm was carrying his great coat,
She, upon hers, a heavy-laden basket;
When, lo! a blast of wind comes, and the man,
Attempting to put on his coat, lets fall
Out of his mouth, ah, misery! his cigar;
But the compassionate woman quickly sets
Her basket on the ground, and with her right hand
Helping the coat on, with the left picks up,
And puts into her own mouth, the cigar,
And whiffs, and keeps it lighting, till the man's
Ready and buttoned up, then gives it back,
And takes her basket, and, all right once more,
Away they go, the man with his cigar,
The woman with the man, well pleased and happy.

"Adam the goodliest man of men since born
His sons, the fairest of her daughters Eve."
PARADISE LOST, IV, 323.

SO father Adam was his own born son,
And her own fairest daughter, mother Eve:
And father Adam was his own sons' brother,
And sister of her daughters, mother Eve.
And father Adam of himself was father,
And mother of herself was mother Eve:
And father Adam was his own grandfather,
And great grandfather, and great great grandfather,
And great great great grandfather—without end:
And mother Eve was her own grandmother,
And great grandmother, and great great grandmother,
And great great great grandmother—without end.
But mother Eve was father Adam's wife,
And father Adam's sons were mother Eve's,
So mother Eve was father Adam's mother,
And grandmother of father Adam's sons,
And grandmother of father Adam's self,
And great grandmother, and great great grandmother,
And great great great grandmother—without end.
And father Adam—being the lawful husband
Of mother Eve, and father of her daughters—
Was mother Eve's own father and grandfather,
And great grandfather, and great great grandfather,
And great great great grandfather—without end.
And mother Eve was father Adam's sister,
Aunt and grand-aunt and niece and cousin-german;
And father Adam, mother Eve's own brother,
Uncle, grand-uncle, nephew, and full cousin.

And father Adam was his own sons' cousin;
And cousin of her daughters, mother Eve:
And father Adam's sons and mother Eve's
Daughters were cousins, all, among each other,
And, intermarrying had sons and daughters,
Goodliest of whom was still old father Adam,
Fairest of whom was still old mother Eve.

ONCE on a time I made a great acquaintance—
Say rather, a great man made my acquaintance—
It was in Rome, that city of great men;
A duke he was, they called him My lord Duke,
And bowed before him, for he was a duke.
Well! though he was a duke, he had heard of me,
And, though he was a duke, desired to see me,
And forced an introduction through a friend
—A duke may have a friend who has a friend
Who has a friend who knows a printer's devil,
Or devil of a printer or bookseller
Or publisher, who in the way of trade's
Acquainted with an author—and came to me,
And shook me by the hand, and on the sofa
Sat down beside me, and, when he had sometime
Stared at me, as a child stares at a lion
Or great white bear in a menagerie,
Began to question me, what? how? where? when?
And was it possible I was so learned,
So very learned as he had heard I was
But scarcely could believe, I looked so simple?
And begged to know their titles that he might
Purchase, and in his library put, my books;
And hoped I would allow him to come often
And chat with me on literary subjects,
When I had leisure and was so inclined;
And did so much regret he could not pay,
This time, a longer visit, but, next time,
I might count on his staying; and away
Went, gracious smiling, and so flattered left me,
That, had I been a dog, I had licked his hand
And wagged my tail, to show my obligation—
And of my lord Duke I heard never more.

So ended in the same hour it began
—Brief, brilliant, phosphorescent, meteoric,
Like a star shooting in the midnight sky
And swallowed up by darkness the next moment—
The only patronage to my lot fell ever
In this great world, where all things go by favor,
And even the king himself not by desert
But favor holds his crown: REX, DEI GRATIA.

[King, by the grace of God]

Inscription on an Egg

DESPISE me not because I am an egg,
A plain, unostentatious, simple oval:
Omnia ex me; and birds, beasts, reptiles, fishes,
Whatever in its nostrils has life's breath,
Even thou thyself—I care not who thou art—
And every tree that grows, and flower that blows,
All, all are brothers of the Dioscuri.

[Castor and Pollux, born of Leda's egg]

A TAP came to my bedroom door, one day,
As, in a fever, sick I lay, in bed,
Restless, desponding, every moment worse:—
"Who's there? come in," said I, and Death came in,
And shook his dart. I put a good face on 't,
But fairly own, I wished him out again.
Once, twice Death shook his dart, and the third time
Had raised, and was in the very act to strike,
When to the door another tap came sudden,
And breathless burst into the room the doctor,
And parried skilful, with gold-headed cane,
Death's thrust, and saved me—saved me, as I thought
And grateful cried out, handing him his fee.
"That fee is mine," said Death, and clutched it fast,
"Or should be mine—my well-earned, just-due fee,
For saving thee—not now indeed, for now
I'm baffled for the moment, but next time,
And not far off's next time—for saving thee
From sickness, pain and sorrow, and the doctor."
I stared; the doctor stared; upon his heel
Death turned about, and, muttering, stumped down stairs.

WE, though a little word of two short letters,
A most important word is, and ambiguous;
Sometimes it means those personages mighty,
The speaker, active, and the passive hearer,
Taken apart, distinguished from mankind.
Sometimes it means the author and his reader,
Pair never without honor to be mentioned,
By me, at least, who in myself comprise,
Not seldom, both the units of this dual,
Writing what no one reads except myself.
In olden time it was a royal word,
This little *We*, and, ungrammatical,
Took on it to express the Lord's anointed,
The DEI-GRATIA DUX, the great bell-wedder.
Those were the glorious days of pigmy *We*,
Too happy to last long, for minor folk,
Following—as minor folk are apt to do—
The bad example set them by their betters,
*We*ed and re-*we*ed and *we*ed again, audacious
And at nought setting decency no less
Than grammar. Whereat kings and queens, incensed
And with disgust filled, cast the plural off
And left it there, to be thenceforth for ever
The representative pronominal
Of editors, reviewers, costermongers,
Tailors and grocers, and hoc genus omne
Of varlets, and to unsophisticated,
Plain, simple *I*, in royal sulk, returned;
And *I*, this moment, our most gracious Queen
Victoria writes herself; *I*, to her lords

[*leader by the grace of God*]

168

And gentlemen in parliament assembled,
Herself addresses. Long may she so write,
Long so address herself—God save the Queen!
Prays *I*, in duty bound and in good grammar.

Anniversary of my mother's death

FOR what our pleasures, and our pains for what,
But occupation till Decay's slow hand,
Assiduous, shall have made sufficient room
Among our foresires' crowded bones for ours?
Full fifteen years ago this very day,
The longest lived of two loved parents died—
Their first born child's place should be nearly ready.

*TWO hundred men and eighteen killed
    For want of a second door!
Ay, for with two doors, each ton coal
    Had cost one penny more.

And what is it else makes England great,
    At home, by land, by sea,
But her cheap coal, and eye's tail turned
    Toward strict economy?

But if a slate falls off the roof
    And kills a passer-by,
Or if a doctor's dose too strong
    Makes some half-dead man die,

*At ten o'clock on the morning of Thursday, January 16, 1862, the great iron beam of the steam-engine which worked the pumps of the Hester coal pit near Hartley in Northumberland, snapped across, and a portion of the beam, 40 tons in weight, fell into the shaft, tearing away the boarded lining so that the earthy sides collapsed and fell in, filling up the shaft in such a manner as not only to cut off all communication between the interior of the pit and the outer world, but entirely to obstruct all passage of pure air into, and of foul air out of, the pit. All the persons who were at work below at the time, two hundred and eighteen in number, were of course suffocated, nor was it until the seventh day after the accident that access could be had to the interior of the pit, or anything, beyond the mere fact of their entombment, ascertained concerning the helpless and unfortunate victims of that 'auri sacra fames' which so generally, so heartlessly, so pertinaciously refuses the poor workers in the coal mines of England, even the sad resource of a second staple or air shaft. See the Illustrated London News of Jan. 25 and Febr. 1, 1862.

We have coroners and deodands
    And inquests, to no end,
And every honest Englishman's
    The hapless sufferer's friend,

And householder's or doctor's foe,
    For he has nought to lose,
And fain will, if he can, keep out
    Of that poor dead man's shoes.

But if of twice a hundred men,
    And eighteen more, the breath
Is stopped at once in a coal pit,
    It's quite a natural death;

For, God be praised! the chance is small
    That either you or I
Should come, for want of a second door,
    In a coal pit to die.

Besides, 'twould cost a thousand times
    As much, or something more,
To make to every pit of coal
    A second, or safety door,

As all the shrouds and coffins cost
    For those who perish now
For want of a second door, and that's
    No trifle, you'll allow;

And trade must live, though now and then
    A man or two may die;
So merry sing "God bless the Queen,"
    And long live you and I;

And, Jenny, let each widow have
    A cup of congo strong,
And every orphan half a cup,
    And so I end my song,

With prayer to God to keep coal cheap,
    Both cheap and plenty too,
And if the pit's a whole mile deep,
    What is it to me or you?

For though we're mortal too, no doubt,
    And Death for us his sithe
Has ready still, the chance is small
    We ever die of stithe.

And if we do, our gracious Queen
    Will, sure, a telegram send,
To say how sore she grieves for us
    And our untimely end;

And out of her own privy purse
    A sovereign down will pay,
To have us decently interred
    And put out of the way;

And burial service shall for us
　　In the churchyard be read,
And more bells rung and more hymns sung
　　Than if we had died in bed:

For such an accident as this
　　May never occur again,
And till it does, one door's enough
　　For pumps, air, coal, and men;

And should it occur—which God forbid!—
　　And stifle every soul,
Remember well, good Christians all,
　　Not one whit worse the coal.

Index of titles and first lines